STUDENT UNIT GUIDE

AS Business Studies

UNIT 3

AQA

Module 3: External Influ... and Objectives and Stra...

John Wolinski

For my parents.

Philip Allan Updates
Market Place
Deddington
Oxfordshire
OX15 0SE

Tel: 01869 338652
Fax: 01869 337590
e-mail: sales@philipallan.co.uk
www.philipallan.co.uk

ISBN 0 86003 456 9

This guide has been written specifically to support students preparing for the AQA AS Business Studies Unit 3 examination. The content has been neither approved nor endorsed by AQA and remains the sole responsibility of the author.

Printed by Information Press, Eynsham, Oxford

Contents

Introduction

About this guide

This Student Unit Guide has been written with one objective in mind: to provide you with the ideal resource for your revision of AQA Unit 3, AS Business Studies. After this introductory note on the aims and assessment of AS, the guide is divided into two sections: Content Guidance and Questions and Answers.

The first section offers concise coverage of Module 3, combining an overview of key terms and concepts with an identification of opportunities for you to illustrate the higher level skills of analysis and evaluation. The scope for linking different topic areas is also shown.

The second section then provides five questions, all focused on a specific area of content and in the same order as the first section. Question 6 is integrated, with a heavy weighting towards SWOT analysis. Each question is based on the format of the AS papers and is followed by two sample answers (an A-grade and a lower-grade response) interspersed by examiner comments.

You should read through the relevant topic area in the Content Guidance section before attempting the question from the Question and Answer section, and only read the specimen answers after you have tackled the question yourself.

The aims of the AS qualification

AS business studies aims to encourage candidates to:

- develop a critical understanding of organisations, the markets they serve and the process of adding value
- be aware that business behaviour can be studied from the perspectives of a range of stakeholders including customers, managers, creditors, owners/shareholders and employees
- acquire a range of skills, including those involved in decision-making and problem-solving
- be aware of current business structure and practice

Assessment

AS and A2 papers are designed to test certain skills. **Every mark that is awarded on an AS or A2 paper is given for the demonstration of a skill.** The content of the course (the theories, concepts and ideas) is there to provide a framework to allow students to show their skills — recognising the content on its own is not enough to merit high marks.

The following skills are tested:

- **Knowledge and understanding** — recognising and describing business concepts and ideas.

- **Application** — being able to explain or apply your understanding.
- **Analysis** — developing a line of thought in order to demonstrate its impact or consequences.
- **Evaluation** — making a judgement by weighing up the evidence provided.

Module 3 (AS External Influences and Objectives and Strategy) has a much higher weighting than Modules 1 and 2 for the 'higher level' skills of analysis and evaluation. Bear this in mind during your preparation and revision for Module 3, as you will need to practise developing arguments more fully for this paper. This will be good practice for the A2 papers that, in general, have a higher weighting for these skills. The units have been designed to allow you to develop these skills as you progress through the course.

The weightings for this paper exactly match the overall weighting for the A-level (25% for each of the four different levels of skill). For this reason, on the basis of skills only, this paper can be said to be the best guide to your overall performance in the A-level. However, a typical A-level student improves his or her skills during the 2 years of the course, and so the grade achieved at the end of the first year in this paper may not accurately reflect the final grade.

Preparation for this unit must be different — the ability to demonstrate knowledge and application is less important (25% weighting rather than the 33% weighting in Modules 1 and 2). Analytical skills are similar in weighting (25% rather than 23%). The major change is in **evaluation** where the weighting is increased from 10 to 25%. Consequently, most questions require some evaluation (judgement). (For Units 1 and 2 only one part of each question requires this skill.)

Practise the specimen questions included in the Question and Answer section of this unit guide. This should be included as a part of your revision plan and will help you to discover the different needs of this paper.

The examination paper for **Module 3** should be weighted so that, on average, marks for each question are awarded as follows:

	Weighting	
Knowledge	10	how well you know the meanings, theories and ideas
Application	10	how well you can explain benefits, problems, calculations, situations
Analysis	10	how well you develop ideas and apply theory and ideas to matters
Evaluation	10	how well you judge the overall significance of the situation
Total	40 marks	

Module 1 (AS Marketing and Accounting and Finance) and **Module 2** (AS People and Operations Management) have an identical weighting for skills. These papers are weighted so that, on average, marks for each question are awarded as follows:

	Weighting	
Knowledge	10	how well you know the meanings, theories and ideas
Application	10	how well you can explain benefits, problems, calculations, situations
Analysis	7	how well you develop ideas and apply theory and ideas to matters
Evaluation	3	how well you judge the overall significance of the situation
Total	30 marks	

The skills requirement of a question

A rough guide to the skills requirement of a question is its mark allocation. In the case of Module 3 (90 minutes), 84 marks are available (including 4 marks for 'quality of language'). For individual questions the mark allocation is as follows:

2–4 marks	a definition or description showing **knowledge**
4–10 marks	an explanation or calculation showing **application**
7–12 marks	development of an argument in the context of the question showing **analysis**
12–20 marks	a judgement of a situation or proposed action showing **evaluation**

In the assessment of 'higher level' questions requiring analysis or evaluation, marks will also be given for the other skills. Factual knowledge displayed, for example, will earn marks for **knowledge** (content) and explanations and calculations will be awarded **application** marks.

In this module it is not possible to recognise immediately the skills requirement by looking at the mark allocation. A better guide to the skills requirement of a question is to look at the trigger word introducing the question. **Specific trigger words will be used to show you when you are being asked to analyse or evaluate.** For AS these will be restricted to the following:

Analyse
- 'Analyse...'
- 'Explain why...'
- 'Examine...'

Evaluate
- 'Evaluate...'
- 'Discuss...'
- 'To what extent...?'

If these trigger words are missing on an AS paper, you are being asked to show 'lower level' skills, i.e. knowledge of the specification content or application (explanation).

Students who fail to **analyse** generally do so because they have curtailed their argument. The words and phrases below serve to provide logical links in an argument. By using them you can demonstrate your ability to analyse.

- 'and so...'
- 'but in the long run...'
- 'which will mean/lead to...'
- 'because...'

In order to **evaluate**, you need to demonstrate judgement and the ability to reach a reasoned conclusion. The following terms will demonstrate to the examiner that this is your intention.

- 'The most significant ... is ... because...'
- 'However, ... would also need to be considered because ...'
- 'The probable result is ... because ...'

It is worth noting when studying for Module 3 that questions involving the interpretation of numerate data and definition questions will be limited.

The style of the examination paper is a case study. Within the specification, the main area that lends itself to interpretation of data is Section 12.1 on *Economic opportunities and constraints* which includes data on issues such as unemployment and inflation. Most of the other sections do not contain reference to issues that include numerate data, thus limiting the scope for numerate questions.

Although it is vital that you understand terms such as 'inflation', 'ethics' and 'SWOT', the fact that 'higher level' skills are being tested means that questions needing definitions will be severely limited.

Opportunities for evaluation in Module 3

The greater focus on evaluation in this unit compared to the other two AS units means that 25% of all marks are awarded for evaluation. Consequently, the specification provides many opportunities for both analysis and evaluation. Examples of these opportunities are listed at the end of each passage in the content guidance section of this book.

Revision strategies

Below is a list of general pieces of advice for exam preparation.

- Prepare well in advance.
- Organise your files, ensuring there are no gaps.
- Read different approaches — there is no one right approach to business studies. Experience as many views and methods as possible. Read newspapers and business articles.
- When reading an article, try to think of the types of question an examiner might ask and how you would answer them. Remember, some of your examination questions will be based on actual organisations.
- Take notes as you read. These will help you to:
  - put the text into your own words, cementing your understanding
  - summarise and emphasise the key points
  - focus your attention
  - précis information which could help with future revision
  - boost your morale by showing an end product of your revision sessions
- Develop and use your higher level skills. Make sure that your revision is not dominated by factual knowledge only. Check that you can explain and analyse the

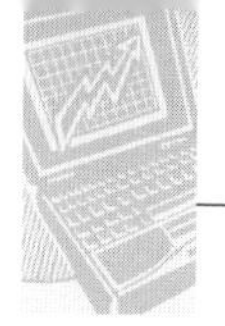

points noted, and try to imagine situations in which evaluation can be applied.

- Practise examination questions. Use the questions in this book (and past papers if available) to improve your technique, making sure that you complete them in the time allowed. In the examination you must complete all questions set on one case study in 90 minutes.
- Maintain your motivation. Reward yourself for achieving targets, but do not get demoralised if you fall behind. If necessary, amend your objectives to a more realistic level.
- Find out the dates and times of your examinations and use this to prepare a detailed schedule for the study leave/examination period, making sure you build in time for relaxation and sleep.
- Focus on all areas of the specification rather than just your favourite topics. Your revision is more likely to 'add value' if it improves your understanding of a problem area. Revising a topic that you already know is a morale booster, but is it as valuable?
- Top up your memory just before the examination. If there are concepts, formulae or ratios that you find difficult, revisit them just before the examination.
- Adopt your own strategy. Everyone has a different learning style — use one that works for you.

Content Guidance

This section of the guide outlines the topic areas of Module 3 which are as follows:

- Economic opportunities and constraints
- Governmental opportunities and constraints
- Social and other opportunities and constraints
- Starting a small firm
- Business objectives
- Business strategy

Read through the relevant topic area before attempting a question from the Question and Answer section.

Key concepts

Key concepts are either defined or shown in bold. You should also have a business studies dictionary to hand.

Analysis

Under this heading there are suggestions on how topic areas could lend themselves to analysis. During your course and the revision period you should refer to these opportunities. Test and practise your understanding of the variety of ways in which a logical argument or line of reasoning can be developed.

Evaluation

Under this heading general opportunities for evaluation are highlighted within particular topic areas.

Integration

The AQA specification states that External Influences should be studied by looking at their influences on business decisions covered in Modules 1 and 2. Objectives and Strategy draw together all other modules, and should be seen as integrating themes which emphasise the interactive nature of the business world. Thus, all topics in Module 3 may need to be combined with elements from other AS modules.

Economic opportunities and constraints

The market and competition

Market conditions

The table shows the different types of competition within which businesses operate.

Feature	Perfect competition	Monopolistic competition	Oligopoly	Monopoly
Number of firms	Many	Many	Few	One *
Product	All the same	Differentiated	Differentiated	Unique
Example	Stock market	Insurance	Chocolate	Post Office — letters
Effect on business	Price takers. Cost efficiency needed for survival. No real scope for marketing. Very low profit margins. Easy to enter or leave the market.	Some influence on price. Cost efficiency very important. Low profit margins. Some benefit from marketing. Easy to enter or leave market.	Non-price competition. High spending on promotion. High profit margins but higher overheads. Aim to achieve USPs through branding. Barriers to entry. Collusion between firms.	Will set price. High profit margins. Can become complacent. Attempt to maintain barriers to entry. Power will depend on importance of product/service and its alternatives.

* When investigating possible use of 'monopoly power', the government defines a monopoly as a firm with more than 25% of the market. This definition would apply to many oligopolists too.

Fair and unfair competition

The table shows that the more competitive the market, the less opportunity there is for profit. A general rule of thumb used by the government in investigating 'unfair competition' is the existence of 'supernormal' profit (profit that is well above the amount that could be 'reasonably expected').

'Unfair competition' is a subjective term. The award of a patent to a company guarantees it a monopoly for a number of years as a reward for the R&D undertaken. In this case, a high profit in one year may just be paying back costs from earlier years. Is it unfair to set a high price if people are prepared to pay it? The answer is more likely to be 'yes' for water supply than it is for a Manchester United shirt.

Examples of unfair competition

- Using an integrated product in a way that denies other companies the opportunity to compete (e.g. Microsoft using its Windows operating system to make it difficult for consumers to access other firms' Internet servers).
- A monopoly charging excessive prices because of the lack of competition.
- Oligopolists agreeing to restrict supply and fix high minimum prices.
- Market-sharing agreements — firms agreeing to operate as local monopolies by not challenging potential competitors in certain geographical areas.
- Restrictions on retailers, e.g. only supplying retailers if they guarantee not to stock rival products or only supplying if the retailer agrees to stock the complete range of a firm's products (full-line forcing).

The significance of the level of capacity in the market

Spare capacity in a market means that the maximum possible output of firms in the market exceeds the demand for the products.

Capacity shortage exists when the demand for the product exceeds the maximum possible supply/output of firms.

Spare capacity	Capacity shortage
• Low prices as companies need to sell their brands. • High fixed costs per unit, leading to higher average costs. • Lower profit margins. • Restructuring of the company to dispose of surplus assets (e.g. labour or land). • Greater focus on marketing needed. • Diversification into new markets. • Firms leaving the market.	• High prices as demand exceeds supply. • Low fixed costs per unit and thus lower average costs. • Higher profit margins. • Investment programmes in order to acquire new fixed assets to increase capacity. • Less need for marketing. Consolidation in existing market. • New firms entering the market.

Analysis Opportunities for analysis in this area include:

- assessing how profitability is affected by the market
- analysing factors that create certain market conditions
- comparing objectives and strategies under different market conditions
- assessing the causes or consequences of spare capacity/capacity shortage
- analysing situations involving possible examples of unfair competition

Evaluation Opportunities for evaluation in this area include:

- evaluating the implications of different market conditions for a firm's success
- judging the influence of market types on a firm's objectives and/or strategies
- discussing the significance of different factors that might be creating capacity shortage or spare capacity

- studying the impact of capacity shortage or spare capacity in a given case
- concluding whether competition is fair or unfair

Links Possible links to other areas include:

- The impact of market conditions on corporate aims and objectives.
- SWOT analysis — opportunities or threats provided by the market.
- The need to adapt the marketing mix to the market situation (e.g. non-price competition in oligopoly markets).
- Product life cycle lengths will depend on the level of competition. In fact, most marketing strategies and tactics link to the market condition.
- Economies of scale will normally be more accessible for monopolists than firms in perfect competition, but less likely if spare capacity exists.

Macroeconomic issues — the business cycle and unemployment

The business cycle (or trade cycle)

The business cycle is the regular pattern of upturns and relative downturns in output and demand. A common description of the stages is shown in the diagram below.

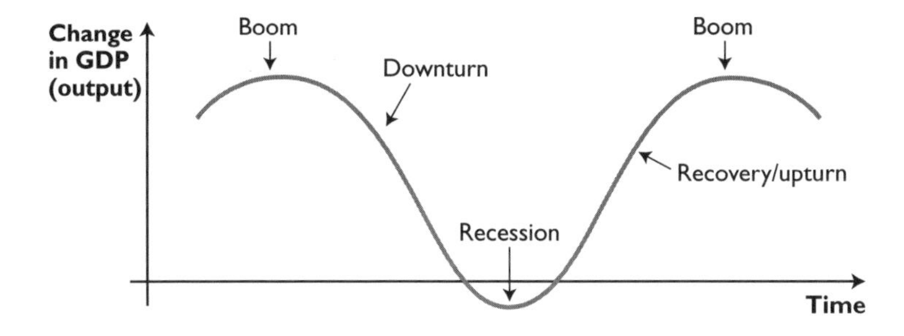

Potential causes of the cycle

- Changes in business confidence, leading to more dramatic changes in investment in fixed assets.
- Periods of stockbuilding or destocking.
- Government policies such as 'stop-go' which aim for growth prior to elections and necessitate applying anti-inflationary measures soon after them.
- Irregular patterns in consumer expenditure on durables influenced by factors such as security and confidence and interest rates.

The implications of the different stages (**boom**, **downturn**, **recession** and **recovery/upturn**) for the organisation are outlined overleaf.

Boom

- Demand exceeds supply ⟶ Prices rise
- Shortages of resources ⟶ Costs rise
- High capacity utilisation ⟶ New investment
- Overall increase in profit ⟶ High retained profits and dividends

Downturn

- Excess stocks ⟶ Need to cut some prices
- High inflation/costs ⟶ Reduces profit and confidence
- Government anti-inflation measures ⟶ Downturn in demand

Recession

- Fall in output and expenditure ⟶ Low profits or losses made
- Liquidations ⟶ Fewer suppliers or consumers
- Bad debts ⟶ Tighter credit control and thus less trade
- High unemployment ⟶ Switch in demand towards inferior goods
- Low investment ⟶ Disproportionate decline in capital goods firms

Recovery/upturn

- Rise in demand for consumer goods ⟶ Some increase in profit
- Time lag before capital investment ⟶ Uneven pace of recovery for different firms
- Business confidence growing ⟶ More investment; more borrowing
- Potential bottlenecks ⟶ High costs if there are shortages

Unemployment

Unemployment can be **cyclical** or **structural**.

Cyclical unemployment is caused by the overall fall in demand that tends to occur during the downturn or recession stages of the business cycle. The impact will vary according to the product or firm.

- Growth products are likely to overcome the effects of recession.
- Inferior goods may gain popularity as people cut back on luxuries.
- In theory, luxury products will decline for the above reason, although people who can afford luxuries are not so likely to become unemployed during a recession.
- Products on low profit margins may suffer as price becomes a more important element of the mix.
- Capital goods and construction firms are likely to experience most problems as business confidence falls.

Structural unemployment is caused by demand or supply factors that apply to a particular industry. Examples include:

- the fall in demand for coal as it was replaced by other fuels
- UK textile firms failing to remain competitive due to low wages in other countries
- lack of competitiveness arising from other factors (e.g. poor reputation)
- technological changes

Implications of unemployment

- Consumer incomes fall, leading to lower sales and thus redundancies.
- Resource suppliers have weaker bargaining power and so raw material prices fall.
- Workers have less bargaining power as alternative jobs are harder to find, leading to lower wage levels.
- Cost-saving exercises will be undertaken, creating cost efficiencies but possible future problems through reduced training and wider spans of control.
- Cutbacks in investment for the future will lead to a further decline in employment.
- Diversification or takeovers and mergers may be used in order to rationalise.

Any desired change in policy may be threatened by the lack of finance available.

Analysis Opportunities for analysis of the trade cycle and unemployment include:

- examining the different causes of one or more stage of the business/trade cycle
- analysing the consequences of the business cycle stage on a particular organisation
- studying the impact of changing stock levels or capital investment or expenditure on consumer durables
- examining the different causes of unemployment in a particular situation
- analysing the implications of unemployment on a particular organisation
- showing how different elements/areas of a firm's activities (e.g. a product or department) may be influenced by unemployment

Evaluation Opportunities for evaluation include:

- judging the relative significance of the different causes of business cycle stages
- demonstrating how recession/boom etc. will have a different impact on different products or organisations
- assessing the relative significance of the different causes of unemployment in a particular situation

Links *Every* action taken by an organisation is directly or indirectly influenced by the business cycle or the level of unemployment. Booms create optimism in business planning; recessions tend to cause pessimism.

Macroeconomic issues — inflation, interest rates and exchange rates

Inflation

Inflation means an increase in price levels. (Deflation describes a decrease in price levels.)

The retail prices index

The retail prices index (RPI) measures inflation. Each month the government studies

the prices of 'a typical cross-section of goods and services' that represent the spending of an average family. The average price change (weighted to take into account the percentage of spend on each good) shows the rate of inflation (or deflation).

Causes of inflation

- **Demand** — if people are prepared to spend more money on products, then prices rise. This is usually caused by increases in consumers' incomes, but can also be the result of a willingness by customers to borrow more money.
- **Costs** — rising costs of raw materials, wages or other expenses result in companies increasing their prices in order to maintain profit levels.
- **Money supply** — prices rise if more money circulates without output rising.
- **Expectations** — if there is an expectation that prices will rise, demand will increase in the short term (before prices rise), so causing inflation. Also, consumers anticipating price rises will be more prepared to pay higher prices.

Implications of inflation

- Higher prices may mean lower sales.
- The international competitiveness of UK firms will be reduced.
- Workers and suppliers will demand higher wages/prices.
- Future uncertainty will mean less reliable forecasts and plans.
- If the government or the Bank of England takes action it is likely to cause higher interest rates and pressure to cut demand and sales.
- Inflation encourages borrowing (but not if interest rates exceed inflation).

Interest rates

Interest rates show the cost of borrowing money, although they can also represent the reward paid for lending money. Loss of interest payments can therefore be seen as the opportunity cost of spending money.

Implications of a rise in interest rates

- Sales of products bought on credit will fall as repayments will be more expensive.
- Saving will be more attractive than spending, causing a further drop in sales.
- People with a mortgage will have less money. The UK has the second highest percentage of people with mortgages in Europe, so this effect is significant.
- There will be less investment for the future as the return on projects is less likely to exceed the interest payments that could be received.
- A rise in the cost of working capital will result in a desire to cut stocks.
- More international savings will be made in sterling to benefit from the interest rate, causing dearer exports but cheaper imports.

Exchange rates

The exchange rate is the price of one currency in terms of another. An **increase** in the exchange rate will result from the following:

- an increase in demand for a currency (caused by an **increase in exports**)
- a decrease in the supply of a currency (caused by an **decrease in imports**)

- high interest rates attracting savings from abroad
- speculation in favour of a currency (caused by speculators expecting a rise in value)
- foreign multinationals buying the currency in order to invest in that country
- governments buying that currency in order to support its value

Types of exchange rates

Flexible or **freely floating exchange rates** exist when the exchange rate is set by supply and demand (mainly based on imports and exports). Governments will not intervene to change the value. In theory, sterling is freely floating.

'Dirty' floating occurs when a floating exchange rate is influenced by government action in order to prevent it changing to an undesirable level.

Fixed exchange rates exist when the value of one currency is fixed against another. For example, 11 EU member countries fixed their exchange rates in preparation for the introduction of the euro on 1 January 1999.

Implications of changes in exchange rates

- An **increase** in the exchange rate means **dearer** exports but **cheaper** imports.
- A **decrease** in the exchange rate means **cheaper** exports but **dearer** imports.
- **Any change** in exchange rates makes it impossible for a company to predict the volume or the price received from its overseas transactions. This discourages trade as it increases the level of risk. Buying currency in advance at a guaranteed, fixed rate helps, but this costs money and therefore reduces profits.

Note: exports and imports also depend on other factors, including reputation and quality, after-sales service and reliability, design, desirability of the product, the overall package provided and payment terms.

Analysis Opportunities for analysis in this area include:

- demonstrating the causes of inflation
- showing how inflation affects a particular organisation's policies
- examining the reasons for a change in interest rates
- studying the implications of changes in interest rates on an organisation
- analysing the implications of fixed and/or flexible exchange rates
- showing how exchange rate changes affect an organisation

Evaluation Opportunities for evaluation include:

- recognising how price elasticity of demand will influence the effect of inflation
- discussing how the cause of inflation can have different implications for a company
- evaluating how interest rate changes affect durable goods, such as cars and furniture, more than smaller items that are not bought on credit
- evaluating the significance of exchange rate changes according to whether the firm is an exporter or importer; the importance of price relative to other factors; the percentage of company activity involving trade; which countries it trades with (recently the pound has risen against the euro but fallen against the dollar)

Governmental opportunities and constraints

UK and EU law

The focus here is on:

- **The reasons for legislation.** In general terms legislation in this area is intended to:
  - protect those with weaker bargaining power, e.g. employees in a large firm or small firms negotiating with a large, powerful trade union
  - ensure that UK firms meet the needs of customers in a cost-effective way which leads to international competitiveness
- **The implications of legislation.** Legislation reduces the possibility of a firm exploiting its customers through unfair activities. It also allows governments to ensure that social factors (externalities) are considered in decision-making. Higher prices (but better products) may result from the legislation.

Health and safety

The aim of health and safety legislation is to provide a safe working environment for employees. The Health and Safety at Work Act (1974) provides the basis and states that firms must provide a safe environment, a written safety policy and training. However, employees must take responsibility for their own and others' safety.

EU directives control working hours, workers lifting heavy weights or using computer screens, and the rights of pregnant workers.

Implications of health and safety legislation

- Extra costs — safety measures, training and employment of safety staff.
- Reputation — a lack of safety could damage sales and recruitment.
- Motivation — security is seen as a factor that can avoid demotivation.

Employment

Employment protection falls into two categories: **individual employment law** and **collective labour law**.

Individual employment law

This legislation aims to ensure that employers and employees act fairly in dealing with others. Key legislation includes:

- Equal Pay Act, 1970
- Sex Discrimination Acts, 1975 and 1986
- Race Relations Act, 1976
- Disability Discrimination Act, 1995

Collective labour law

This legislation aims to control industrial relations and trade union activities. Various pieces of legislation cover the following:

- Contracts of employment — employees must receive a contract within 13 weeks if employed for more than 16 hours per week.
- Notice of dismissal — after 4 weeks of work an employee is guaranteed 1 week's notice, increasing to 1 week for every year employed up to a maximum of 12 weeks.
- Dismissal procedures — all employees must be told about the formal procedures that must be followed by the company.
- Trade union activities, e.g. rules on picketing and strikes.

Consumer protection

Consumer protection legislation aims to safeguard consumers from exploitation or exposure to unsafe products or services. Legislation, overseen by the Office of Fair Trading (OFT), includes:

- Sale of Goods Act, 1979 — goods must be fit for the particular purpose, of merchantable quality, as described.
- Weights and Measures Act, 1963 and 1985 — weights and measures must be accurate and displayed.
- Trade Descriptions Act, 1968 — adverts must be truthful and accurate.
- Consumer Credit Act, 1974 — limits the giving of credit to licensed brokers/ organisations.
- Consumer Protection Act, 1987 — companies are responsible for damage caused by their products.
- Food Safety Act, 1990 — controls the safety of food products.

In addition there are voluntary controls, monitored by the industry or through an independent body such as the Advertising Standards Authority (ASA).

Implications of consumer protection

- Increased costs of production.
- Potential savings on rectifying problems.
- Improved quality and thus enhanced reputation and consumer loyalty.

Competition policy

This aims to limit the power of firms to take advantage of monopolies, mergers and restrictive practices. Competition should lead to better quality, cheaper products and to increasing international competitiveness.

Ways of safeguarding against such exploitation include:

- The Competition Commission — this body ensures that firms with significant market share (or proposed mergers) do not act against consumers' interests.
- Watchdog organisations such as OFWAT and OFGAS — these were set up to prevent privatised companies from exploiting their customers.

- Greater competition — forcing government bodies to contract out services to the best bid, in order to prevent excessive pricing and poor service.
- Reducing restrictive practices — taking measures to prevent actions (such as cartels) that limit competition and customer choice.

Implications of competition policy

- Lower prices for customers.
- Lower profit margins for companies.
- Greater incentives for firms to seek competitive advantage through 'fair' rather than 'unfair' competition (e.g. by creating cheaper or innovative products).

Analysis Opportunities for analysis include:

- investigating the reasons for government legislation
- showing how a company needs to adapt its strategy to a change in legislation
- analysing the impact of government actions on an organisation or particular situation
- examining the pros or cons of an area of government or EU law

Evaluation Opportunities for evaluation include:

- evaluating the relative merits of different forms of legislation
- discussing the impact of laws on a particular organisation
- arguing the overall case for government intervention of this type

Social and other opportunities and constraints

Social responsibilities

Social responsibilities are the firm's duties towards society in the form of stakeholders. The key requirements of the various stakeholders are summarised below.

Stakeholders	Key requirement of stakeholder
Employees	Secure, reasonably paid employment.
Customers	Good quality, safe products at a competitive price.
Suppliers	Fair prices and regular custom and payment.
Owners	Good profit leading to increases in share prices and/or dividends.
Government/society	Efficient use of resources and also consideration of the environment and society's needs.
Local community	Employment and wealth creation without imposing major social costs.

From the firm's perspective, being socially responsible has the following benefits:

- it improves image, meaning higher sales
- it encourages greater brand loyalty, allowing higher prices
- it makes it easier to recruit the best workers and motivate staff

A firm which accepts its social responsibilities can face the following problems:

- socially responsible policies can be costly to introduce
- a culture change within the company may be necessary
- adopting these policies will cause conflict between stakeholders
- social costs and benefits are not always easy to identify, e.g. Monsanto saw GM crops as a way of eliminating the problems of plant disease

The table below sets out **the arguments for and against social responsibilities**.

Arguments for	Arguments against
• Problems such as unemployment and pollution will be reduced. • The quality of life will be improved as decisions will be based on what is best for society rather than what is best for one firm. • Business wealth can be used to help society. • Morally, individual organisations should do the right thing. • Society's long-term needs can be considered when a business might focus only on the short term.	• The efficient use of resources may be reduced if businesses are restricted in how they can produce and where they can locate. This will cause higher prices. • International competitiveness will be reduced if other countries do not consider externalities. • Stakeholders will always have different views. • Social responsibility is subjective and is much harder to measure than clear profit targets. • Business managers may lack the skills to deal with such issues.

Business ethics

Ethical behaviour is subjective. In broad terms, ethical behaviour is behaviour that is seen to be morally correct. Examples of ethical issues include:

- Should a firm relocate to a country paying lower wage levels?
- Should a firm release a life-saving drug after limited testing?
- Should private health care organisations train doctors and nurses?
- Can organisations, such as Railtrack, balance profit and safety?
- Should companies practise positive discrimination?
- Should advertising aimed at children be restrained?
- Should working hours be limited?

The pros and cons of ethical behaviour are similar to those shown under social responsibilities (above). A further issue is the implementation of an ethical policy.

The following points highlight the possible **difficulties** firms could face when deciding whether to adopt an ethical policy.

- **Effect on profit** — an ethical choice can incur extra costs, e.g. buying renewable resources from a less developed country; continuing extensive testing of a product before release; failing to introduce products that do not meet ethical standards.
- **What is ethical?** People have different views on what is ethical and these change over time. An example of this in Britain is Sunday trading.
- **Communication of ethics within the organisation** — in large organisations it may be difficult to inform staff of the policy and to monitor adherence to it.
- **Delegation and empowerment** — as empowered workers take more decisions, it becomes harder to maintain a company policy on ethical behaviour.

Analysis Opportunities for analysis in this area include:

- examining the level of social responsibility shown by a firm
- showing how a more socially responsible (or ethical) policy can be implemented
- analysing why a firm might want to become more (or less) socially responsible
- demonstrating the consequences of a particular ethical or socially influenced decision
- analysing the conflict between profit and ethics
- showing how different stakeholders take varying stances on these issues
- examining the impact of delegation on ethical decision-making

Evaluation Opportunities for evaluation in this area include:

- making a judgement on the key social/moral issues influencing policy
- assessing the desirability of balancing social and other needs
- evaluating the impact of different stakeholder needs
- monitoring the extent to which social and ethical decisions depend on other factors such as the market and competition
- contrasting the short-term and long-term implications of social responsibility.

Technological change

Technology is constantly advancing. Areas of technological change include products and services, production processes, operating methods and materials.

The **benefits** from new technology to society, firms and consumers are:

- **Improved efficiency and reduced waste** — cost-effective use of the world's resources benefits consumers and firms, and in the long run resources last longer.
- **Better products and services** — company profits are increased and consumers benefit from better choice.
- **New products and materials** — needs and wants that were previously not satisfied are provided for.
- **Advances in communication** — company efficiency is increased and consumer needs are met more directly.
- **Improved working environments** — employees work in safer conditions and there are greater number of jobs which are less physically-demanding and more interesting.

- **Wealth creation** — higher living standards are achieved.

The **problems** of introducing new technology are:

- **Cost** — the need to remain up to date can lead to very high replacement costs on a more regular basis.
- **Knowing when and what to buy** — in rapidly changing markets an investment in technology that is about to be dated can be an expensive mistake.
- **Industrial relations** — with technology replacing jobs there is a danger of resistance by workers and a lowering of morale.
- **Personnel** — new skills are required with implications for recruitment, retention and training costs.
- **Breakdowns** — where processes become dependent on technology, breakdowns can cause major disruption and therefore expense.

Firms may experience **resistance to changes** in technology for a number of reasons:

- Some people have a natural tendency to resist change.
- Employees may recognise that individually they will suffer from a change, even if the firm as a whole benefits.
- Employees may not recognise the benefits (they may have received no explanation).
- Stakeholders will view the implications differently. For example, a customer might see a better product, whilst the local community might see job losses.
- Workers can have different values. One worker may value the improved pay; another may regard the lower job security as more significant.

Analysis This area lends itself to an analysis of the extent of the benefits to a business. As new technology (unless restricted by a patent) is available to all organisations, the benefit depends on the degree to which competitors can match the firm.

Products

- In the short term, benefits arising from new products may be very significant. Consumers will pay premium prices for a unique product.
- This 'supernormal' profit can remain if a patent can prevent competition. However, there will probably be 'me-too' products that reduce the uniqueness of the original.
- Companies can use this period to develop the next, unique product.
- In a monopolistic market, the lack of competition will allow companies to continue to make high profits, thus limiting the incentive to introduce new, improved products.
- In some industries, the high cost of new technology acts as a barrier to entry, allowing organisations to keep profit high in the long run.

Processes

- New technology can improve the efficiency of processes. In the short term, this may help a company to raise its profit margins.
- In a competitive market this advantage will soon disappear as new firms adopt these processes too, causing margins to decrease.
- In the long run, the profit will rise through greater sales volume as the lower price will make the product accessible to more customers.

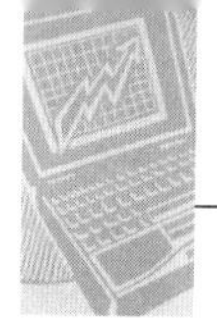

Other issues for analysis in this area could relate to the following points:

- The adoption of new technology will be influenced by existing technology. Is it compatible? Can the changeover in methods be managed?
- Reaction of the workforce to new technology — the cooperation of employees will be needed.
- Stress — any change brings with it a period of stress and companies need to monitor the signs of stress if they wish to ensure a smooth transition.

Evaluation This topic lends itself to evaluation as a range of issues can be introduced. In any given scenario there needs to be a reasoned judgement balancing the benefits of new technology (usually new markets and customers) against the problems created (usually personnel and operational issues). Other considerations are finance (problems in the short term but benefits in the long term) and the reliability of projections. It is impossible to be totally sure of the impact of changes.

Starting a small firm

Identifying an opportunity

Given that approximately one third of all new businesses fail in their first 3 years, an entrepreneur has to think carefully about the logic behind a new business. Business opportunities can take a number of forms:

- **Using existing skills** — a firm based on the existing skills and understanding of the owner should benefit from this individual's awareness of the market and interest in the tasks. The main problems are likely to be the marketability of the idea.
- **Identifying a gap in the market** — assuming the firm attracts sufficient customers, does the owner have the necessary skills to meet their needs profitably?
- **Purchasing a franchise** — this is a tried and tested idea which limits the risk of the owner. However, it also limits profitability and the franchisee may be vulnerable if the franchisor has not researched the possibility carefully.
- **Invention or innovation** — inventors who start a firm on the strength of a new invention have the benefit of a market niche but the possible problem of being product-led rather than market-led.

Protecting ideas

The methods below allow a firm to retain its unique appeal by preventing direct copy. However, for very small firms the costs may be too high.

- **Patents** — provide inventors with exclusive rights to make a product for 16 to 20 years.

- **Registered design** — a form of protection which prevents copy of designs for a period of up to 15 years.
- **Trademarks** — indicated by the symbol ®. They take the form of a symbol or style of wording that cannot be copied by rivals.
- **Copyright** — indicated by the symbol ©. It applies to printed material such as a book that cannot be copied directly.

Research and marketing with small budgets

Research can be carried out using the following methods and resources:

- the *Yellow Pages* or local business directories to show what is offered and where.
- market mapping — this can show a gap in the market for a product or service that is not being provided at all
- other secondary sources — census data or local government data
- primary research — limited direct research or information gleaned from listening to local people (e.g. complaints about leaky garage roofs on a particular estate)

Marketing can be carried out via the following:

- leaflet distribution personally or through a local newspaper or distributor
- posters in shop windows
- advertisements in the local newspaper, possibly with special offers
- local business directories or the *Yellow Pages*
- specialist magazines relevant to the product (these may be national)
- public relations (PR) — arranging events that will achieve newspaper coverage
- word-of-mouth — comments from satisfied customers are a major form of marketing for a new firm

Practical problems of start-up

The potential problems that start-ups can encounter are shown in the table below.

Finance	Marketing	Operational	Personnel	Personal
• raising funds • cash flow • profitability • investment	• deciding on the product • forecasting sales • target market • market research • price competition • forms of promotion	• suitable premises • location • production methods • sources of supply	• recruitment • selection • training • structure	• suitability for self-employment • cover for illness • opportunity cost

Analysis Opportunities for analysis include:

- examining the qualities needed by an entrepreneur
- analysing the marketability of the product or service
- considering the importance of other internal issues that determine success
- analysing the impact of external factors
- assessing the feasibility, advantages or weaknesses of a business plan

Evaluation This topic lends itself to evaluation. Scenarios can be created in which a number of factors will determine the success or failure of a business start-up. Evaluation may consider:

- why a start-up failed
- why a new business succeeded
- the measures that a firm should take
- the degree to which the owner could have prevented failure (or contributed to success)

Legal structure

Limited or unlimited liability?

There are two broad categories of business, **incorporated** and **unincorporated**.

Unincorporated

In an **unincorporated** business there is no distinction in law between the individual owners of a business and the business itself. Such businesses are in the hands of sole traders or partnerships. *(No understanding of partnerships is required for the AQA A-level in business studies.)*

In the eyes of the law, an individual must pay his or her debts to any creditors in full. This concept is known as **unlimited liability**. Any debts that the business owes must be paid out of the funds of the owner.

Incorporated

An **incorporated** business has a legal identity that is separate from the individual owners. In the private sector these are private limited companies (Ltds), public limited companies (PLCs) and cooperatives, mutuals or friendly societies. (*No understanding of cooperatives, mutuals or friendly societies is required for the AQA A-level in business studies.*) These firms can own assets, owe money and enter into contracts in their own right as they are recognised legally as a separate entity.

A feature of incorporated businesses is **limited liability**. The liability of these firms is limited to the fully paid-up share capital. So, if the business goes into liquidation the owners (shareholders) have no responsibility for further payments if they have already paid for their shares. Legally the business has 'died' and so its debts 'die' with it.

Forms of business ownership

The forms of business ownership covered by AS are:

Sole trader — a business owned by one person. He or she may employ staff. Sole traders are most commonly found in the provision of local services.

Private limited company (Ltd) — funded by shares that cannot be advertised for sale without the agreement of the other shareholders. This means that second-hand shares cannot be sold on the stock exchange. As a result, they are limited in size.

Public limited company (PLC) — funded by shares. PLCs must issue at least £50,000 of shares, and their shares can be advertised. Most try to secure a stock exchange listing allowing their second-hand shares to be bought and sold easily.

The **advantages and disadvantages** of these types of businesses are shown below.

Type of business	Advantages	Disdvantages
Sole trader	• Easy and cheap to set up. • Very flexible to changes in circumstances. • Owner takes all of the profit (and thus there is strong motivation). • Independence. • More privacy than other firms.	• Unlimited liability. • High risk and limited collateral for loans. • Limited capital. • Organisational difficulties (holidays and illness). • Limited skills.
Private limited company	• Limited liability. • More capital than sole traders. • More privacy than PLCs. • More flexible than PLCs.	• Shares less attractive because they are difficult to sell. • Less flexible if expansion needs finance. • Legal formalities compared to unincorporated firms.
Public limited company	• Limited liability. • Easier to raise finance. • Greater scope for new investment. • Can obtain economies of scale. • Stock exchange listing acts as a guarantee of stability.	• Must publicise performance. • Greater scrutiny of activities. • More administration. • Founders of firm may lose control of ownership.

The divorce between ownership and control

Traditionally entrepreneurs have two functions:
(1) Taking risks (by providing finance) — **ownership**.
(2) Making decisions (managing the organisation) — **control**.

In a sole trader business, the owner and manager are likely to be the same person so these functions remain with that one person (the entrepreneur).

However, in PLCs, the owners (shareholders) vote for directors who appoint managers to make the decisions. In this case, the two functions of ownership and

control are divorced (separated). These functions have become split because:

- The growth of firms has led to many limited companies expanding beyond their original owners (e.g. a Ltd company becoming a PLC) in order to compete.
- Large PLCs have attracted shareholders who only wish to earn dividends or capital gains but do not want to be involved in management.
- Additional wealth has led to more people acquiring the finances needed to purchase shares.
- Deliberate government policy has widened share ownership.

However, two trends have limited the extent of this divorce:

(1) The growth of small firms in recent years.

(2) The decline of public ownership.

Implications of a divorce

- It is easier for companies to acquire more finance.
- Managers can be selected on merit rather than share ownership.
- There is a greater conflict of interests, with managers taking decisions that may not suit the needs of the owners.
- Shareholders find it difficult to access the information needed to challenge or judge the quality of managers' decisions.
- Shareholders take a narrow focus on short-term finances as they have less understanding of the needs of other stakeholders.

Analysis and evaluation The descriptive nature of this element limits the scope for analysis and evaluation. The main opportunities exist in contrasting the relative merits of different forms of ownership (particularly the choice facing a person in a given situation); commenting on the merits of limited liability; and evaluating the causes or implications of the divorce between ownership and control.

Business objectives

Corporate aims and goals

Corporate aims

These are the long-term intentions of an organisation. The aims, sometimes in the form of a **mission statement**, provide a general focus from which more specific objectives can be set.

Corporate objectives (or goals)

These are medium- or long-term goals that provide a more measured, specific translation of the aims, allowing an organisation to measure the level of achievement of its aims. The **purposes of objectives** are to:

- provide direction
- unify staff
- measure and improve efficiency
- motivate staff
- pinpoint strengths and weaknesses and allow action to be taken
- monitor the relevance of activities
- communicate to stakeholders

Good objectives will be **SMART**:

Specific **M**easurable **A**ttainable **R**ealistic **T**imed

Typical corporate objectives are laid out in the table below.

Objective	Analysis
Survival	A key objective for most small or new firms. More significant during periods of uncertainty and recession. Important in competitive markets.
Financial	Profit-maximising in theory, but more likely to be satisficing (a satisfactory level of profit). Short-term profit may conflict with long-term profit. Break-even will be the target for mutual societies, friendly societies and public services. Profit target must be adjusted to the business environment and so it will be influenced by the level of competition, existence of spare capacity, stage of the business cycle, demand for the product etc.
Growth	A popular objective because it is easy to measure. Less likely for small businesses that value independence. Affected by the external factors noted above.
Corporate image (reputation and image/product quality)	Pride of the owners may lead to this being a key objective. Likely to help other objectives such as growth and profit. Will vary according to the customers' needs — a quality image will appeal to consumers who buy on the basis of quality rather than price. Image depends on the market segment — 'cheap and cheerful' may be the best reputation in a certain market. The level of competition will affect the need for a positive image.
Meeting the needs of other stakeholders	Many organisations place a high value on considering the needs of others in their corporate objectives (this can also enhance reputation). Examples are: • providing good working conditions, pay, opportunities and training for workers • environmental priorities — ensuring that products and processes do not damage the environment • social awareness — providing for the needs of the local community and disadvantaged sectors of society

Long-term or short-term objectives

Objective-setting can be seen as an early stage in business decision-making. Decisions need to be made in the context of the firm's overall aims. However, in practice, objectives are constantly modified in the light of market changes, levels of achievement and future opportunities.

In general, the achievement of long-term aims will be a dominant influence on a company's actions. On occasions, short-term objectives may vary from the long-term aims for the following reasons:

- **Financial crisis** — this will encourage a firm to look towards survival rather than growth or profit.
- **New competition** — long-term needs might encourage a firm to modify its policy in order to eliminate a rival. For example, destroyer (or predator) pricing might be used for a short time until the competition is eliminated and price can be increased again.
- **Economic conditions** — in a recession, greater emphasis will be placed on survival; in a boom, the potential for high profits may encourage other targets such as helping the environment or local community, or diversification.
- **Government policy** — changes (e.g. in employment policy) may force a company to adopt different priorities.
- **Image changes** — recent negative publicity may encourage a firm to focus on improving its image in the short term in order to re-establish itself in the market.
- **Management style** — the owner may prefer to focus on the immediate future.

Analysis The table on page 29 highlights the factors that influence the actual objectives chosen by an organisation. Further potential for analysis includes:

- examining the reasons for objectives
- considering reasons for adopting short-term objectives
- analysing the quality of a specific objective
- recommending suitable objectives for a given organisation
- showing the links between objectives and company policies
- looking at the implications for companies/departments of switching between short-term and long-term objectives

Evaluation Opportunities for evaluation include:

- demonstrating the degree to which objectives are appropriate to a firm
- evaluating the different influences on a firm's objectives
- judging the actions of a company in the context of its objectives
- discussing the merits and suitability of an organisation's objectives
- evaluating the relative merits of short- and long-term objectives in a particular situation

Stakeholders

Traditionally, firms were established by their owners to meet the needs of those owners. Business aims and objectives were therefore dominated by the needs of the shareholders (the owners). This approach is known as the **shareholder concept**.

Over the years, a number of organisations took a different view by prioritising the needs of other groups (e.g. the John Lewis Partnership meeting the needs of employees; the Co-operative Society satisfying customer needs). Governments have also restricted corporate decisions in order to meet the wider needs of society by considering externalities arising from those decisions. Theorists, notably Charles Handy, have supported the view that firms should take the initiative in meeting the needs of these other **stakeholders**.

A stakeholder is an individual or group with an interest in an organisation's performance.

Common and conflicting aims

A company should try to serve the needs of these groups or individuals, but whilst some needs are common, other needs conflict.

Even within a stakeholder group there may be conflicting aims — some customers will favour low prices whilst others will favour quality. The list below summarises the possible requirements of each stakeholder group in terms of their objectives.

Shareholders

- high profit secured by cheap costs or high prices
- high dividends
- long-term growth to support share prices
- cost-effective production
- positive corporate image

Staff (workforce)

- job security and good working conditions
- high pay
- labour-intensive production

Customers

- low prices
- high-quality products
- good service
- invention and innovation
- choice

Suppliers

- regular custom, prompt payment and reasonable prices for materials
- growth, leading to more orders in the future

Residents

- employment prospects
- safeguarding the environment
- acceptance of social costs such as noise and water pollution

The state

- employment
- reasonable prices
- efficient use of resources
- compliance with legislation on consumer protection and competition policy
- compliance with legislation on employment and health and safety

Analysis Opportunities for analysis include:

- explaining how and why different stakeholders listed above would prioritise their aims
- demonstrating the common aims of different stakeholder groups
- analysing the conflict between the aims of different groups
- assessing the impact on a company changing from the 'shareholder concept' to a consideration of all stakeholder needs
- explaining how a company benefits from serving the needs of different stakeholders

Evaluation Opportunities for evaluation include:

- discussing the relative importance of different stakeholders in a particular case
- evaluating the circumstances in which the views of individual groups will be considered
- judging the degree of common ground and/or conflict between different aims
- evaluating the types of aims or objectives that a firm should pursue in order to meet its stakeholder needs

Business strategy

SWOT analysis

SWOT analysis is a system that allows an organisation to assess its overall position, or the position of one of its divisions, products or activities. The analysis looks at the **internal factors** within the company that influence its position. These are:

- **S**trengths
- **W**eaknesses

External factors that might influence the position of a business are described as:
- **O**pportunities
- **T**hreats

Areas that could be assessed in a SWOT analysis vary from organisation to organisation, but some aspects that are likely to be included are outlined below.

Internal factors

- reputation or corporate image
- quality of product
- level of innovation
- brands and product portfolio
- understanding of the market
- skills of personnel
- recruitment, selection and training
- attitudes and turnover of staff
- fixed assets and investment
- research and development levels
- location
- company structure
- operational methods
- profitability
- liquidity

External factors

- stage of the business cycle
- local economic conditions
- degree and type of competition
- actions of competitors
- developments within the market
- government economic policy
- legislation
- accessibility of new markets
- extent of change
- technology
- social and political trends
- demographic changes
- pressure group activity

SWOT analysis is the application of these and other factors to a particular organisation (or element of that organisation) in order to assist planning. An example of a SWOT analysis drawing on the internal and external factors above is shown in the table overleaf.

Internal factors

Strengths	Weaknesses
Excellent reputation for high-quality products.	Reputation as a poor employer.
High-quality products.	Product portfolio has too many products in decline and growth stages, with a shortage of products in maturity.
Seen as innovative.	Expertise in a limited range of market segments.
Highly skilled staff, selected through a well-organised recruitment process.	Limited provision of training for office staff and production line workers.
Sound investment in fixed assets and modern equipment and methods.	High levels of staff turnover and absenteeism.
An international leader in research and development in its field.	Poor accessibility to location of main headquarters.
An efficient, delayered company structure.	Communication difficulties between different divisions and subsidiaries.
Very profitable in comparison to similar organisations.	Low level of liquidity and cash flow problems in recent years.

External factors

Opportunities	Threats
Low wages and high unemployment levels locally amongst staff with appropriate skills.	Downturn predicted in the business cycle.
Main competitor experiencing financial difficulties.	High levels of competition within the market.
Government economic policy is encouraging more spending.	Many new products are being released by new entrants into the market.
Recent legislation will require many companies to buy one of the industry's pieces of equipment.	Technological changes mean that recent capital purchases will become obsolete soon.
New markets opening up in other parts of the world.	An ageing population will mean fewer sales of certain products.
Social trends will encourage families to purchase more of certain products.	Pressure group activity against the opening of new factory.

Evaluation Although SWOT is described as analysis, it also involves evaluating the relative importance of the causes and/or consequences of the strengths, weaknesses, opportunities and threats.

Questions & Answers

In this section of the guide there are six questions. Each question is followed by two sample answers interspersed by examiner comments.

Questions

The questions are based on the format of the AS papers. This unit (External Influences and Objectives and Strategy) differs from Units 1 and 2 in that **much greater weighting is given to evaluation**. Consequently, most questions will be evaluative, and those that do require evaluation will carry more marks for evaluation than the other skills such as knowledge, application and analysis. Look out for the key words or phrases that show that evaluation is required. These are: '**evaluate**', '**discuss**' and '**to what extent ...?**'

Tackle the questions in this book to develop your technique, allowing yourself 90 minutes to answer all parts of each question. By considering the specimen answers provided and the examiner comments you will be able to see how these questions may be answered effectively and identify (and so avoid) the potential pitfalls.

A common problem for students (and teachers) when completing a topic is the lack of examination questions that cover only the topic in question. These questions have been tailored so that students can apply their learning whilst a topic is still fresh in their minds. **Questions 1 to 5** are focused on a specific area of content covered in the same order as the Content Guidance section of this guide. These questions may be tackled during the course or on completion of the revision of that particular content area. (Please note that question 2 on UK and EU law includes 'the market and competition' from the first section of the specification. You will therefore need to have covered this before attempting question 2.) **Question 6** is integrated, with a heavy weighting towards SWOT analysis. Remember, you will always be given credit for using business concepts from outside a unit, as long as their inclusion and use is relevant to the question.

Sample answers

Resist the temptation to study the answers before you have attempted the questions. In each case, the first answer (by Candidate A) is intended to show the type of response that would earn a grade A on that paper. An A grade does not mean perfection — these answers are intended to show the range of responses that can earn high marks. In business studies, it is the quality of the reasoning that is rewarded. Candidate B's answers demonstrate responses that warrant a pass, but not at the A-grade level.

Examiner's comments

The examiner's comments are preceded by the icon e. They are interspersed in the answers and indicate where credit is due. In the weaker answers, they also point out areas for improvement, specific problems and common errors.

Economic opportunities and constraints

Study the information and answer **all** parts of the question that follows.

www.hm-treasury.gov.uk

Hilary waved a piece of paper in front of Bob. 'Good news on the whole, I would think.' It was April 2000 and the paper was an extract of the economic indicators for March 2000, published on the government's Web site. Bob scrutinised the summary:

Unemployment	5.9% of the workforce	(a fall of 0.4% since March 1999)
RPI	Increase of 2.3% per annum	(1999 rate = 2.7% per annum)
Interest rates	6.0%	(a rise of 0.25% on the previous month)
Exchange rate for sterling	Average increase of 9.0% since 1997	
Overall investment	Increase of 3.8% in last year	
Manufacturing investment	Decrease of 13.3% in last year	

'The summary doesn't mention the business cycle, Hilary,' observed Bob.

'The business cycle is in an upturn at the moment,' replied Hilary. 'The unemployment is structural rather than cyclical. It's actually 9.3% in our region — much higher than the national rate of 5.9%. There were worries about a recession caused by the decrease in manufacturing investment and companies cutting back on their stock levels. However, those problems didn't happen and as you can see, overall investment has risen. It is only manufacturing investment that has fallen.'

Blake Holdings plc had been a success story in the 1990s. Originally, the company had imported novelty products from other countries, mostly in Eastern Europe and Asia, operating purely as a retailer. However, some difficulties with products that failed to meet UK legislation had led the company to open a factory in which it modified foreign products for the UK market. Soon this had become its main business, and Blake Holdings was recognised as the company to contact if you needed to have a foreign product modified to meet British Standards. The Queen's Award for Industry in 1996 added to its growing reputation.

Since 1998, the company had modified its strategy slightly, exporting some of its products to EU countries whose laws demanded the same standards as the UK. This part of the business was expanding, and in 2 years, exports had grown to 20% of annual sales. **The fall in people's expectation of inflation had led to a reduction in the rate of inflation**, which had helped UK exporters.

Bob reflected on the company's success. With 100% of the materials imported but only 20% then exported, the rise in the exchange rate had affected Blake Holdings differently to many other UK firms. Bob pondered the opportunities and constraints offered by the information in the table.

(1) What is the meaning of the 'RPI' (see table)? (5 marks)

(2) Analyse the reasons why 'the fall in people's expectation of inflation had led to a reduction in the rate of inflation'. (10 marks)

(3) (a) Explain the causes of structural unemployment. (6 marks)

(b) Evaluate the implications of a fall in unemployment for a company such as Blake Holdings. (14 marks)

(4) Discuss the effect of the increase in interest rates shown in the table on Blake Holdings. (15 marks)

(5) Discuss the impact of lower investment and a fall in stock levels on the business cycle. (15 marks)

(6) To what extent has the increase in the exchange rate contributed to the company's success? (15 marks)

Total: 80 marks

■ ■ ■

Answer to question 1: candidate A

(1) Retail prices index.

> *e* This is correct, but not informative enough. The wording of the question means that the use or significance of the RPI is needed too.

(2) Inflation is caused by many factors. 'Cost-push' inflation comes from a rise in costs, like wages, raw materials and machinery. If any of these increase, a company will increase its prices to avoid making a loss.

> *e* A worrying start. Has the candidate realised that the question is about falling inflation?

Another type is called 'demand-pull'. Here the demand for something goes up, and if demand goes up firms can increase their prices.

The question asks about inflation falling. For prices to fall, the opposite to the above must be taking place. Costs of raw materials will be falling. The government might have cut VAT. It is unlikely that wages would have caused it as they do not tend to fall, especially in countries with strong trade unions.

> *e* It is now obvious that the question has been read. The candidate has shown the common misconception that falling inflation rates mean a fall in prices. Lower inflation rates mean that prices are still rising, but not so quickly as before. However, the business logic being shown is good and so this would not be penalised. A nice sentence on wages (although higher productivity can cut the wage bill per unit).

Once prices start to fall, people will think carefully before buying something. If they wait to buy then it might be cheaper. If everyone waits then the demand will be lower and prices will be cut by firms which will be desperate to get rid of their supplies. It then becomes a vicious circle. If prices fall it will mean that raw materials will be cheaper, and so cost-push inflation falls, making prices cheaper again. Companies will now save on their costs and cut prices again.

The answer develops and concludes well. There was an opportunity to make greater reference to company expectations when setting prices here, but this is a good answer to a tricky question.

(3) (a) Structural unemployment is caused by firms becoming uncompetitive. In Britain, the coal industry is an example. It is also caused by a lack of demand. If people stop buying cars then jobs will be lost in the car industry. The solution is to retrain people or get other industries to move to the region where the jobs have been lost.

Factually correct, but no explanation is offered for the first point and there is a minimal development of the second. The final sentence looks at solutions rather than causes, and so adds no value to the response.

(b) Unemployment will affect Blake Holdings in two main ways. First, demand will fall as people have less money when they are out of a job. If people are worried about their jobs (which they will be if unemployment is high) then this will also mean that they cut back on spending. A fall in unemployment will have the opposite effect, so Blake Holdings should increase its sales.

It is vital that the question is read carefully and planned beforehand. Always check during an answer that you are keeping to the question. This question refers to a fall in unemployment, and not a rise. The last sentence of this paragraph retrieves the situation and so full credit can be given to this paragraph, but the next argument reverts back to high unemployment. In this area of the specification it is vital that you can argue on any change in a variable, according to the question set. All the same, some credit would be given for the logic shown.

It will save on costs too. A period of unemployment is usually linked to lower prices. Wages can be reduced as workers will want to keep their jobs. It all depends on the products that it makes.

The final sentence could have led on to genuine evaluation. As a starting-point it shows good technique, but the lack of any further comment shows that it is not a genuine evaluation. Adding 'because ...' might have led to a good conclusion.

(4) An increase in interest rates will affect the company in a number of ways. First, it will make borrowing more expensive. This will make costs rise and lead to higher prices. If the market is very competitive the company will lose a lot of sales, but for its novelty products this may not be too important.

The unique nature of the product might mean that it could pass the increase in costs on to the customer. It would also depend on gearing — if the company is highly geared the interest rate would affect it much more, but a low-geared company would not be affected.

question

e A nicely structured answer that looks at two key issues. The paragraph on borrowing is first rate, with evaluation being shown in the nature of the product and the gearing (although this latter element was not developed so well).

The increase is only 0.25% and so any change is likely to be small for any of the factors looked at.

e Excellent. This one sentence shows a sharp sense of awareness and excellent use of the data.

Second, it will affect sales. High interest rates make it more expensive to borrow and so consumers will buy less because their mortgages will cost more. This will particularly hit firms making cars and durables, because consumers borrow money to buy them. I would think that Blake's products fit into this category as they would need to be expensive to make it worthwhile to import and modify. Sales might plummet. Higher interest rates would also increase the value of the pound.

e Good use of context again, although the penultimate sentence in this paragraph is rather extreme.

(5) The business cycle shows the ups and downs of the economy. Typically, over a period of time, there will be an upturn leading to a boom, and then a downturn leading to a recession, and then on to a recovery or upturn again. Governments will usually try to stop the downturn turning into a recession.

e Very good: the candidate demonstrates that the concept is clearly understood.

If there is lower investment this will lead to a recession or downturn because firms are buying fewer units of machinery, and so firms which make machinery will cut back on production. A recession is when output falls. These firms will cut back on jobs and so unemployment will rise. Job losses will make things worse because workers will have less money to spend.

Investment depends on business confidence. As the recession gets worse, firms will cut back on their investment even more as they do not want machines making things that no one will buy. They will also have less money to buy them, and banks will be less willing to lend money if demand is falling.

e Nice analysis. The logic has been extended well to show the long-term consequences and the interconnection between customers and suppliers.

Stock levels will have a similar effect. Companies which cut back on stock levels may be worried about future sales, and if they stock less it will mean fewer sales (even if this is only caused by customers not being able to buy because no stock is available). Suppliers of stock will cut back on production, causing a downturn in the trade cycle. Some companies, though, may just be changing their policy. A company introducing just in time might cut its stock levels for a different reason.

e A good observation that presented an opportunity to evaluate by showing how the fall in stock levels might not inevitably affect the business cycle. Unfortunately, the opportunity was not taken.

(6) An increase in exchange rates is bad news for a company. If exchange rates rise then it will be much harder to export products and so Britain's balance of payments will become worse. Unemployment will rise and so companies will want to change this because they do not want to cause these problems for the country. It might be bad for their image and lead to a loss of profit.

e The point raised in the third sentence is valid, but companies will rarely consider their impact on the whole economy — they have more focused aims.

The exchange rate has increased by 9%. This is a big increase and may mean that the business will have to close down.

e The conclusion is extreme. There is no context to this answer and it seems that the candidate has left too little time to answer this question.

e **Despite the final part, this script would reach the grade A standard. In earlier answers the candidate uses the data well and the economic ideas have been logically developed throughout. In places, the answers would have benefited from less certainty and more appreciation of the shades of grey that exist. The answers to parts (2), (4) and (5) are very strong.**

■ ■ ■

Answer to question 1: candidate B

(1) It means the retail prices index. This measures the rate of inflation. It looks at the price of a typical basket of goods each month, and works out how much prices have changed.

e A very comprehensive answer which would earn full marks. It shows the value of clear language in achieving a full explanation without wasting precious time.

(2) Inflation is caused by prices rising. Ingredients and raw material costs will cause inflation; it might be wages. If costs rise then prices will go up.

e The candidate starts by falling into the trap of answering the question that he or she wanted, rather than the one set.

People spending more money will put prices up too. As people get richer they will spend more and so companies will increase their prices. If a person thinks that a price will rise soon and the shopkeeper thinks so too, then the shopkeeper will put up the price to get the best possible profit.

e The final sentence is lacking in substance, but does begin to address the question and earns some credit.

(3) (a) Structural unemployment is caused by changes in the structure of an industry.

e The candidate is repeating the words in the question, rather than explaining.

If the demand for that product falls because no one wants it any more then firms will sack their workers. This is structural unemployment. An example is the coal industry, as people do not have coal fires any more. Another example is when costs get too high and people buy from other countries. Britain used to make lots of clothes but wages are too high now, compared to places like Asia.

e Again, an effective use of language has meant that a reasonably concise answer has earned high marks.

(b) A fall in unemployment will affect Blake Holdings. Unemployment in the region is high and so it will pay low wages. A fall in unemployment will mean that wage costs will go up and make its products dearer and so it will sell less. However, it will still be paying lower wages than its competitors in other places.

e The candidate has made excellent use of the article to put the answer in the context of the company.

Demand will increase, especially for luxuries like novelty products. As people get richer they spend a bigger percentage of their money on luxuries and so Bob's company should do well. The export side of the business will depend on jobs increasing in other countries.

e A further example of effective use of the data. The answer reads well because it has not been memorised. The candidate understands the logic of the topic and is applying that logic to the situation.

In conclusion, I think that Blake Holdings will benefit, because the increase in demand will outweigh the rise in wages. Most of the costs are spent on buying the products. Modifying them will need machines and so it may be that wages are only a small expense. Blake Holdings will make more profit.

e Drawing a conclusion is a good way of ensuring evaluation, although in this answer evaluation is shown throughout. Overall, a top class response.

(4) Higher interest rates will mean that it is more expensive to borrow money and so consumers will cut back on their spending. This will reduce the demand for products and, as costs will be higher, it will cut profits.

e Sound analysis but no evaluation.

It will increase costs because most firms borrow money or may have an overdraft. If Bob's company has an overdraft it will mean higher interest payments and so the company has to increase the price. This will lead to a further fall in sales.

In the article it mentions that a part of the business was expanding. If the company has borrowed a lot of money for this expansion then the interest rates could be a major problem. Such a big expansion may have come from more shares being sold or from retained profit. In this case the interest rates would not be a problem.

e The second line of argument is dealt with more effectively. There is not always concrete information on which to make judgements and it is valid to describe situations in which a factor becomes more (or less) significant. This answer shows high level skills, albeit rather briefly.

(5) Lower investment means that people are saving less money. People will save less money in the form of shares, which will mean that companies have less money.

e Unfortunately, investment in business means the purchase of fixed assets and so this interpretation is not valid.

A fall in stock levels could be caused by a lack of demand, and so it may mean that there is a recession or a good is out of fashion. It could be because the product is very popular and with everyone rushing out to buy it the stocks have run out.

e This second paragraph looks at cause rather than effect (impact).

(6) The pound has increased by 9% since 1997. This means, for example, that if the pound was worth 10 francs in 1997, it is now worth 10.9 francs. This would make it very difficult to export because a French person would find English products 9% more expensive and so they would buy French products instead (unless they really liked the English product). Blake Holdings exports 20% of its products and so this would not be a serious problem for the company. In fact, it would benefit because it imports 100% of its raw materials.

e A superb treatment of the impact of exchange rates, with the application based on the information relating to Blake Holdings.

These raw materials will be 9% cheaper than they were so its costs will be much lower than rivals who buy English raw materials. In England, the products will be 9% cheaper and with inflation at 2.3% this is a big advantage.

e This argument shows evaluation, but a question starting with the words 'to what extent' will require some comparison to other factors if it is to be answered fully.

I think that this is the major reason for the company's success. However, it is not the only factor. Good marketing is needed and it says in the article that Blake Holdings has a good reputation and won an award. These factors would have helped too.

e Fortunately, the last paragraph does acknowledge other issues, but it would benefit from some comment on their significance.

e **The quality of candidate B's answers was more uneven than that of candidate A's. The simple explanations (1 and 3(a)) were dealt with more effectively, and the answers to 3(b), 4 and 6 used the data well. Unfortunately, questions 2 and 5 displayed weaknesses. Overall, the analysis and evaluation shown would have compensated for the weaknesses and this candidate would have earned a B grade.**

Governmental opportunities and constraints

Study the information and answer **all** parts of the question that follows.

Jim's gym supplies

Jim Stevenson, the managing director of SMET, paused to consider the excited comments of Emily Duport, the marketing manager. 'Emily, I agree that this idea looks like a winner, and that we need to keep researching different markets, but we need to stay focused.'

The original factory (now the engineering components division of SMET) was finding it tough. The market was populated by hundreds of small firms, all producing identical components for the machine tool industry. Fortunately for SMET, Emily had persuaded the board to diversify into the manufacture of fitness equipment. In this market SMET was meeting with much greater success. The firm had gained from the massive growth in this market and had benefited from the fact that SMET was one of only four companies in Britain able to produce the full range of equipment being demanded by the multitude of gyms springing up in every town.

The cause of Emily's excitement was the new 'virtual reality' treadmills. Market research had indicated that the idea would be a winner amongst people who wanted to keep fit in a more enjoyable way. The R&D team had just completed the prototype of a treadmill that kept you exercising whilst experiencing a virtual reality that could be programmed into the machine — it had caused a sensation in the factory and workers were refusing to go home until they had had their go. The invention had been patented, giving SMET a monopoly of the production of this particular machine.

Emily continued, 'We should be changing the products that we offer, as a reaction to our different markets. The degree of competition in each market affects the ability of SMET to make a profit. Should we still be making engineering components?'

Another feature of the fitness equipment market had been the continued existence of capacity shortage, in sharp contrast to the excess capacity that existed in the production of engineering components. Market projections indicated that the situation in the fitness equipment market would not fundamentally change over the next 4 years.

Year	1	2	3	4
Projected demand for fitness equipment	100	120	142	166
Projected supply of fitness equipment	85	100	120	146

Nevertheless, Jim had been frustrated by the firm's inability to persuade the largest leisure company — Lloyd Davids — to purchase SMET's equipment.

'It seems like unfair competition to me: they buy all of their equipment from A1 Artefacts, the market leader. Perhaps our new treadmills will make them change their minds.'

Leroy Winton spoke for the first time. 'As operations director I am worried about this expansion. We have had to make a lot of changes to the factory to comply with health and safety legislation. There have been complaints about unfair dismissals and redundancies in the components division, and the minimum wage has increased our labour costs in the warehouses. There seems to be no benefit to companies from this government interference and I think we should consider a production plant in another country.'

'It's the consumer protection issues that annoy me,' replied Jim. 'I can understand the need to protect individuals, but SMET sells its products to other companies — most of which are much larger than us. Surely they are big enough to protect themselves!'

Emily reminded Jim that he was booked into the virtual reality treadmill in 20 minutes' time. In the next 25 minutes Jim settled four key strategic decisions and shot his first Martian.

(1) What is meant by the terms:

(a) 'fair competition' (4 marks)

(b) 'excess capacity'? (4 marks)

(2) Evaluate strategies that SMET could use in order to benefit from a period of capacity shortage. (18 marks)

(3) To what extent would the degree of competition in a particular market affect SMET's ability to make a profit in that market? (18 marks)

(4) Discuss the impact of employment protection legislation on UK firms such as SMET. (18 marks)

(5) Discuss Jim's view that consumer protection is not required when the consumer is a large firm rather than an individual. (18 marks)

Total: 80 marks

■ ■ ■

Answer to question 2: candidate A

(1) 'Fair competition' means that there is a lot of competition. Sellers are price-takers who cannot take advantage of the consumer by restricting supply or taking over competitors to limit choice. The consumer is king.

'Excess capacity' is like the motor industry at the moment. There are too many factories and so it is possible to build far more cars than the consumers want to buy. It means that prices should fall and could lead to factory closures.

e Two excellent definitions with brief comments to show their significance. These comments would meet the needs of the examiner.

(2) A capacity shortage is the opposite to excess capacity.

e A good start. Defining the term overcomes the potential for irrelevance — particularly important in this case as Question 1(b) would have encouraged candidates to start thinking about excess capacity instead.

If there is a capacity shortage, a firm could benefit from low costs because it will

be using its fixed assets very efficiently. This might allow it to cut prices and force the competition out of the market. I would not advise this strategy though because the Competition Commission might investigate if it became a monopoly (25% of the market). Besides, it will cut profits for a while and it does not need to cut prices to attract customers because of the shortage.

Although the candidate eventually concludes that it is not a worthwhile strategy, this is an excellent line of approach because it allows the candidate to display his or her skills. The critical factor is that the price cut is a *feasible* choice. The logic is presented to show why it could be done, and then judgement (evaluation) is shown in the reasons given for not adopting it.

The company could also increase prices. There is a shortage in the market and only four competitors. This is a golden opportunity for SMET to make money before new firms enter the market. However, it does want to keep the goodwill of its customers and so this might be risky.

The answer is further strengthened by the inclusion and reasoning behind an alternative strategy.

I think SMET should increase its capacity. The capacity shortage is predicted to continue for the next 4 years and it should be able to sell all that it produces. This may enable it to dominate the market if it grows faster than its rivals. In the current situation it could be making a lot of money to fund this expansion.

A brilliant answer, earning maximum marks.

(3) The degree of competition will influence profit. In perfect competition there are lots of small firms all competing fiercely. There are no barriers to entry so new firms will enter the market if profits are being made. This will cut profits.

This is a contrast to the previous response. In question 2, the excellence of the answer came from its use of the context of the case study. Unfortunately, this is a purely theoretical summary of competition and ignores the case study.

Oligopolists will make more profit as long as they avoid price wars. There are only a few competitors, all with different products. Non-price competition occurs here, with strong branding that creates USPs and encourages brand loyalty. If customers buy your products regardless of price you will make more money.

Monopolists make the most money. With no competition they can charge whatever they like and the consumer has no alternative. However, the Competition Commission can investigate them and the privatised monopolies have watchdogs to stop them overcharging.

The theory is good, and credit would be awarded for the lower level skills (but not for evaluation). The view that monopolists can keep putting up prices fails to recognise the importance of the demand for the product in any market.

(4) Employment protection imposes duties on employers that will increase their costs.

Leroy has mentioned how SMET had to spend money on changes in the factory to comply with health and safety legislation. This could lead to higher costs which could make the company uncompetitive. In fairness this is unlikely because most other countries have similar laws and so it should not affect our prices against their prices. It would be important if the products were made in countries that did not have the same laws, such as parts of Africa and South America, but gym equipment is complicated and is likely to be produced in countries like Germany and the USA which will have the same laws.

The minimum wage would have had more of an effect because Britain has introduced it more recently than other countries.

Employment protection may help the company. Unfair dismissals are happening and this would imply that SMET is a bad employer. Legislation that makes the company treat its workers more fairly will improve its reputation and help sales.

It will also help recruitment and retention. If workers see that SMET is providing a pleasant working environment, they will want to stay and are likely to work harder. Herzberg states that poor working conditions will demotivate workers. Legislation on training may help productivity too, and a well-trained happy workforce will make more money for a company.

e The use of the information, and particularly the logical extension of thinking beyond the immediate information given, is first rate. The candidate is answering the question as if he/she were representing SMET and trying to discover the impact.

On balance I think SMET will benefit. Gym equipment is expensive and if the legislation helps the company to have a good reputation and a productive workforce, then it should overcome any expenses that it has to pay.

e The assumptions made are reasonable and the use of points mentioned in the case to illustrate the broader issues is very good. The candidate's use of English shows judgement in its own right, e.g. 'could lead to', 'may help', 'is likely to' in places where the outcome is not absolutely certain (as is so often the case).

(5) To some extent Jim might be right. Consumer protection was introduced to stop exploitation and this is more likely to happen to an individual than a large firm. If a company is unhappy and takes its custom elsewhere, this will have a big impact on the other firm and so it will make sure that it does not upset the large firm.

e A nicely qualified opening paragraph.

However, I think that Jim is wrong. Everybody should be treated equally in a democracy, and it is wrong for a business to see one customer as more important than another one. Consumer protection laws make sure that this happens.

e A potentially dangerous style exhibited: is the answer going to stray away from business issues?

Furthermore, Jim is wrong because of the unnecessary expense that would take

place. If a product is faulty it means an inefficient use of the world's limited resources, and so this waste should be stopped.

Just staying the right side of the divide between business analysis and other issues.

Jim has also ignored the fact that a dangerous piece of gym equipment might injure a customer of the gym, and so it will not be the large company that suffers but someone else (although the gym could be sued). In fact, there is a law that holds companies responsible for problems caused by faulty products.

It is very difficult to see if a product is fit for purpose, as described, or whether it is the correct weight or measure. For this reason, any purchaser is entitled to the same level of protection. It would be a dangerous precedent to set if firms thought that they could get away with poor products. It would not help exporters either, as I am sure that other countries would protect their large firms.

The final two paragraphs are very focused and overall this is a high-quality answer in which the candidate shows that he or she is applying understanding.

This is a high grade A set of answers. In questions 2, 4 and 5, the candidate makes excellent use of the information, even though the nature of some of the questions makes this harder to achieve than in many other topics. The clarity of understanding would also merit high marks in question 1. Only question 3 fails to maintain the standard — the candidate shows good understanding, but the absence of context is a major problem.

■ ■ ■

Answer to question 2: candidate B

(1) 'Fair competition' means that there are many buyers and many sellers in a market.

This is a definition of perfect competition, although it does loosely refer to circumstances in which fair competition exists.

'Excess capacity' means that companies have an excess of capacity — they could produce more products because their production plants are not fully used. They have spare capacity.

No credit for the repetition of the question, but it eventually describes the term well.

(2) During capacity shortage a company would find that demand exceeds supply. This would enable it to change its marketing strategies and its marketing mix.

The opening sentence is sound and it would enable marketing strategies to change (but they are not the only strategies).

The company has a unique product with the new treadmill, and could advertise this in health and fitness magazines, or in places like cinemas where younger people visit. Whilst it is new they could benefit from charging a high price, until 'me-too' products come on to the market.

e The answer drifts away from the question — first by ignoring the reference to capacity shortage, and then on to the new product.

The new treadmill could be made available in exclusive shops to help keep the price high. SMET could also charge higher prices for its other products. If there is a shortage then it will lead to a rise in price. It could also find new places — persuade new gyms to stock the products.

e Only the sentence on 'shortage' is relevant to the question set.

(3) SMET's gym equipment seems to be much more profitable than its engineering components. There are four companies which means that the market is an oligopoly. SMET should be able to make a good profit in this market. There is already a shortage anyway, but with only three other firms SMET may want to set up a cartel. This is where the four companies could agree to fix prices or not invade each other's geographical territories. (Cartels are illegal but difficult to detect.)

e A superb answer, using the data in a logical and productive manner. Evaluation is shown in the bracketed comment on cartels, the link between profit and the scope for high prices, and the view that price wars have short-term effects.

Usually in oligopoly firms use non-price competition to compete. This consists of advertising and promotions so that customers want to buy your brand rather than a rival product. Profits can be kept high by high prices. Price wars will force down profits, but these can happen if a firm wants a larger market share.

The new treadmill has a patent and so this is a monopoly. With no competition SMET may not need to advertise so much and it can charge a high price because there is no alternative. However, there is always an alternative or opportunity cost, and that is to do nothing. In this case, customers can choose not to use the treadmill. The profit will depend on how desperate customers are to use it.

e The section on monopoly contrasts the scope for profit well, with excellent insight being shown by the comment on consumer demand.

It is another story for the engineering components. This is 'populated by hundreds of small firms'. This makes it perfect competition and so there is little scope for profit. Even if a profit is made it will only encourage more competitors who will push down the price.

e The section on perfect competition confirms that this deserves a high mark. A summary at the end to clarify the comparison would have enhanced the response.

(4) Having to obey government rules and laws is a major expense for large companies in the UK. Personnel departments need to keep lots of records for the government.

Valid points but with minimal explanation. The points are very general and only at the end of the answer is there a recognition of SMET's situation.

It makes it difficult to be flexible because you cannot get rid of workers if demand falls, and laws like the minimum wage will increase costs and make it difficult to keep prices down. The company is thinking about moving to another country because of the problems caused by this legislation.

There is a danger inherent in having a strong opinion on a topic, as seems to be the case here. Evaluation requires weighing up evidence and it is unlikely (but not impossible) that all of the evidence will point in one direction.

(5) There are many Acts of Parliament that protect consumers:

Weights and Measures Act: this makes sure that companies do not sell less than they declare on the packet.

Sale of Goods Act: goods must be of merchantable quality, fit for purpose, and as described. This protects consumers from faulty goods, or ones that do not do what they are supposed to do.

Trade Descriptions Act: adverts must be honest and truthful.

The final question has been misinterpreted, possibly because the candidate was expecting a question on the reasons why individuals need consumer protection.

All of these acts prevent companies from taking advantage of customers. This is needed because it is impossible for buyers to know whether a product like a kettle will work until they get it home. If it explodes after 3 weeks, was it fit for the purpose? Consumer protection helps the individual against big business.

Credit would be given for the full understanding of the legislation shown by the candidate, and so this would score on content. There would also be credit for the explanation and analysis of the needs of individuals to receive protection. However, the answer only addresses part of the question and there is no judgement provided.

The candidate had some understanding of the basic ideas, but found it difficult to put them into the context of the questions set. The answer to question 3 was exceptional, but there was no serious attempt to evaluate in any of the other answers. The relatively high marks earned for content, and the quality of question 3, would make this a good D-grade answer overall.

Q3 Question

Social and other opportunities and constraints

Study the information and answer **all** parts of the question that follows.

STAG

It had been a difficult time for STAG. Services To Agriculture (STAG) had been a mutual, non-profit-making society. Originally it had produced and leased agricultural machinery to small farmers who could not afford to purchase expensive equipment. More recently, it had become very difficult to compete with larger producers, and many small farmers could not afford STAG's machinery, despite the organisation's reputation and the loyalty that most small farmers had for it. It was accepted that STAG had to modernise its production methods, with new technology replacing the old machinery. Over time, two other divisions had been formed:

- The insurance division — this had specialised in insurance related to agriculture in its early years, but its insurance provision and customer base no longer reflected its origins. In terms of scale, this division accounted for 70% of the organisation's revenue.
- The consultancy division — this had been established to advise farmers on their impact on the environment and society. Although small, it was the fastest growing part of the organisation.

In the 1990s, the insurance division had suffered financial difficulties, the main cause being the fierce competition from companies offering insurance quotes over the telephone. STAG had maintained its sales force, until 1996.

The need for additional finance to bring new technology into the machinery and insurance divisions had been the key argument proposed by those members who had supported the move to become a PLC in 2000. The extra finance available from shareholders would enable STAG to compete with the larger companies. STAG had only survived because of the quality of its service and the loyalty of its workers and customers. However, consultation with the workforce had revealed differing opinions. Some employees welcomed the new technology. For other workers it had a demotivating effect.

STAG had always prided itself on being a business with strong 'ethical' priorities. In the 1990s, STAG had stayed in business because its overseas investments yielded high profits. Originally, these investments had been in projects that created new jobs in less developed countries, but at the 2000 AGM it was revealed that some of these investments were supporting the policies of an unpopular dictatorship, whilst other investments involved deforestation of the Amazon, and the growing of genetically modified crops. The argument that there was a conflict between the company's need for ethics and the need for profit was not received with great enthusiasm by stakeholders.

The board of directors was eager to reassure customers and staff. The company newsletter proclaimed: 'We shall continue to serve the needs of all our stakeholders. Every strategic decision and all key activities will be scrutinised to ensure that the business is acting in a socially responsible way.'

(1) What is meant by 'business ethics'? (5 marks)

(2) Discuss the potential for conflict between ethical behaviour and profit in STAG. (16 marks)

(3) (a) Analyse the different ways in which STAG could become more socially responsible. (11 marks)

(b) To what extent would the success of STAG be affected by the introduction of a greater degree of social responsibility in its actions? (16 marks)

(4) Evaluate the effects of technological change on staff motivation in the different divisions of STAG. (16 marks)

(5) Discuss the possible opportunities for STAG that might arise from technological change. (16 marks)

Total: 80 marks

■ ■ ■

Answer to question 3: candidate A

(1) Business ethics are a code of practice adopted by an organisation that is seen to be morally correct. This code is not based on legal requirements, but on what society perceives to be correct behaviour. An example of ethical behaviour would be a company agreeing to buy materials to help a less developed country.

e A good definition, supported by an example that confirms that this candidate has a good understanding of the term.

(2) There is always a danger of conflict between ethical behaviour and profits. The example above shows a firm that is paying a more expensive price for materials. Consequently, it is likely to make less profit.

e A good piece of analysis.

Of course, there may not be conflict. Consumers who value ethical behaviour may pay more for a product that is seen to be helping a cause that they believe in. Mostly, businesses will publicise their ethical behaviour — they would not want their kindness to go unnoticed.

e Evaluation shown in this passage.

In STAG's case there has already been conflict and it is going to remain. It had become a PLC in 2000 and now has shareholders who want it to make a profit, but the directors have stated the need for social responsibility.

e Good use of the case to answer the question directly. On occasions there will be obvious clues within the text.

The degree of conflict will depend on profit. If a high profit is made, the shareholders who want profit may not be worried by ethical behaviour. However, if the market changes or the company becomes inefficient, then it might want more effort put into making a profit instead of supporting ethical practices. Few shareholders expect maximum profits. It is much easier to be ethical in a boom.

Excellent argument and development showing the highest skills.

It will also depend on the competition. If competitors are unethical, it will be harder to match their costs but easier to differentiate yourself. Are consumers interested in price or do they want a unique selling point? Ethics will not always cost money, and you may earn goodwill by doing something you would have done anyway.

A full answer worthy of top marks.

(3) (a) STAG could conduct a social audit. An independent expert would analyse the company's practices and report on the level of social responsibility. If weaknesses were found, the company could act to put them right. In the case of STAG, its consultancy division offers the most scope for responsible behaviour. Its expertise in the environment will help farmers to act in a socially responsible way, by not polluting or creating eyesores in the countryside.

Some evaluation shown, although only analysis is required for this particular question.

The insurance division has been getting rid of workers — this is not socially responsible, but if it was necessary for survival then it could be argued that the reorganisation was socially responsible.

The final two sentences show good ideas, but they should be developed a little more.

(b) Using the ideas in 3(a), I will show the effects on STAG's success.

The consultancy division will improve its reputation if it helps farmers to deal with their impact on the environment. It seems to me that the more successful they are in improving the environment, the more customers they will get.

A good, logical structure. This approach guarantees that the focus will be in the context required. The conclusions drawn in the three paragraphs that follow show mature analysis, with judgement being demonstrated in the weighing up of situations, especially concerning the insurance section.

Making and leasing machines for small farmers is socially responsible and gives them a market niche. It does state, though, that it is losing market share.

In insurance, STAG would experience problems if it decided to keep the workers employed. Could it still compete? I do not see how the insurance division could be socially responsible and successful. It could refuse to insure against pollution or force insurers to take measures to prevent noise, pollution and other actions that would upset society. Unfortunately, this might lose business too.

In conclusion, STAG's social responsibility appears to be helping it, except in insurance. If it had stayed as a specialist insurer for agriculture it might have been more immune from competition. It depends on how you measure success — before it became a PLC it would have wanted to break even. Success would have been measured by the quality of service. It is probable that this would still be one of the

measures used — profit would not be the only way of judging success.

A brilliant conclusion, meeting the requirements of a fully evaluative answer.

(4) Technological change can mean job losses, which would demoralise the staff who remained. They would not feel secure and this could affect productivity.

Technological change would mean restructuring of the factory. This would cost money and mean that there is less available for wages and to improve working conditions.

Technological change would increase the efficiency of the firm and this will mean more profit. This is happening in the insurance section and could lead to more pay and job security; both are motivating factors according to Taylor.

The candidate seems to be running out of time. The points made are good and deserve more development. There is no evaluation shown and only a slight reference to the situation in the final sentence.

(5) Technological change can benefit a firm in four ways:

- new products
- new processes
- new methods of operating
- new materials

This structure is logical and is a good template, but it does not guarantee the focus on STAG that is needed. A structure based on the divisions of STAG would ensure focus, but runs the risk of discussing the wrong issues. Either approach would work *as long as a constant eye is kept on the wording of the question.*

The agricultural machinery division might benefit from new products, but it is unlikely that they will discover products that larger producers have not.

The insurance part will benefit a lot from more efficient systems from new technology, leading to more profit to reinvest in new activities. It should also increase its market share.

The final two paragraphs earn credit but need to be developed in the context of STAG's situation.

This was clearly a very good candidate, but the answers were not balanced in the most efficient manner. Questions 1 to 3 earned almost maximum marks, but questions 4 and 5 were too brief. The understanding shown in questions 4 and 5 was good. If time was a problem it would have been better to have spent less time on questions 2 and 3(b). Practising under examination conditions would have secured more time for these final questions. Overall, the answers are still of grade A standard, but not at the very highest level that appeared probable after question 3.

Answer to question 3: candidate B

(1) Ethics means the style of management. It is the way in which the business treats its employees and customers, and whether it is morally justified in its actions.

> The candidate is guessing. This is not penalised because the loss of time is seen as the penalty. In this instance the last suggestion is valid, although too vague to earn a good mark.

(2) If there is Theory X management then workers will do what they are told. Decisions will be taken quickly but the ideas may not be very good as they will all come from the manager. If it treats its customers well it will mean loyal customers who will return again and again. Word of mouth advertising can lead to even more sales. It can also charge a premium price if customers are satisfied.

If it is morally justified in its actions it will also have the same effect. Customers will buy more products and pay higher prices if it approves of the company.

> This answer is penalised for the candidate's lack of understanding of the term 'Theory X'. All of the ideas expressed are irrelevant, until the final line. This secures some marks, but the answer is vague. A lack of precise understanding of concepts in this unit could be very costly. Evaluative questions, worth approximately 16 marks, can only be answered effectively if the basic terms are understood.

(3) (a)
- look after the environment
- increase employment
- buy only renewable resources
- avoid pollution
- limit noise

> A bullet point response. Only content marks (3 or 4 out of 11) can be awarded.

(b) These measures would cost money, but they could help STAG to satisfy its consumers. Looking after the environment would cost money, but there would be laws that need to be obeyed and so they could do this quite cheaply.

Increasing employment would be difficult. If it did this in insurance it would lose money.

Renewable resources are more expensive, but it could use them to gain publicity and boost its reputation.

STAG does not cause pollution and noise, so these are not important.

> A logical approach to use. The answers are brief, but relate well to the case. They do emphasise that the candidate had more understanding than was displayed in 3(a).

In conclusion, I would say that employment will cause the most problems. STAG could not compete with its old workforce, but it does not seem to have much effect elsewhere.

An attempt to evaluate at the end, but clumsy wording and minimal expansion.

(4) Technological change will have lowered morale in insurance as the workers that remain would have lost their friends. They could be feeling insecure — once a company has reorganised it often does it again. It may be more competitive and if the technology improves profits it will mean more job security. Maslow saw this as a motivator (Herzberg saw a lack of security as a demotivator).

A good structure, linking application and analysis.

Technological change is very expensive and this might affect the ability of the machinery division to compete.

Consultancy services are labour intensive. Communications would have been improved by mobile 'phones and portable computers, but the most important motivators are the job itself, responsibility and recognition. Technology does not seem to have changed these factors very much in STAG.

An interesting conclusion. Sometimes there is a temptation to make an issue far more important than it is. The recognition that a factor is not important is a mature judgement. Unfortunately, the answer requires much greater justification and supporting evidence than that presented.

(5) Technological change has helped STAG's insurance division to compete, although it could be argued that it made it uncompetitive in the first place. For a country such as the UK which cannot compete on wage costs, companies will find that technology offers the opportunities to introduce more efficient methods. It can also help them to produce new products for the market.

Good analysis in general, with evaluation shown in this paragraph.

Communications will benefit from new technology and STAG's business would find this helpful. Consultants can benefit from constant access to their office and by access to papers on the Internet. Insurance quotes can be given immediately at any time or place, helping to secure business.

Overall, this is a good grade D answer. Sometimes early difficulties undermine a candidate's confidence, but after a tentative start, this student has persevered and the later questions reflect the candidate's strengths in a way that the first two questions did not. Each question should be seen as a fresh start — no single question will guarantee failure (or success).

Starting a small firm

Study the information and answer **all** parts of the question that follows.

The everlasting sticky tape

Ricky recalled that fateful day, 6 years ago. He could not believe his luck when the Patent Office had told him that nobody had patented the process. He was the first person to present the idea of an 'everlasting sticky tape'. Ricky had registered his patent immediately. On parcels and paper the tape was as effective as normal sticky tape, but once the 'unstick stick' had been rolled across it the tape lost its stickiness. The tape could then be rolled up again and within 24 hours would regain its sticky properties to be used again and again.

The production process was fairly simple, but the small scale of operation meant high costs of production. Ricky wished that he could match the prices of the main tape manufacturers: if only he had access to their production methods and scale.

The first 3 years were difficult, and it was only his savings and Gemma's income that kept the business running. Meanwhile, his friend Alan was earning high profits from his Internet café. The irony was that this had been Ricky's original plan for a business, but the 'everlasting sticky tape' had seemed like such a good idea that he had encouraged Alan to open the café. As Alan pointed out, the café had been so much easier to research and market.

Fortunately, some contacts at the local chamber of commerce eventually led to a significant increase in custom for the everlasting sticky tape, and the fourth and fifth years as a sole trader showed a reasonable profit.

Ricky's accountant had encouraged Ricky to convert his business from its status as a sole trader. The accountant accepted Ricky's fierce desire to be his own boss, but with sales revenue of £500,000 per annum and the drive to move into large-scale production, he was determined to persuade Ricky that it was sensible to convert to a business that offered limited liability. PLC status would attract the funds and expertise to allow Ricky's invention to be produced on a large scale.

Ricky had originally been worried about the divorce between ownership and control that tended to occur in PLCs. A bout of 'flu had finally persuaded Ricky of the wisdom of this advice. Everlasting Sticky Tape PLC was now quoted on the stock exchange. The first year as the managing director had been a steep learning curve for Ricky, but with orders now rolling in he felt secure enough to leave the business in the capable hands of his fellow directors, while he helped to fulfil Gemma's lifelong desire to visit Hawaii.

(1) What is the significance of 'limited liability' for a business? (8 marks)

(2) Explain the reasons for the 'divorce between ownership and control' in a limited company. (8 marks)

(3) Discuss why the market research and marketing of Ricky's business presented a greater challenge than the market research and marketing of Alan's Internet café. (16 marks)

(4) Evaluate the relative merits of the accountant's advice to Ricky to convert from sole trader to public limited company. (16 marks)

question

(5) Evaluate the problems of business start-up faced by Ricky in establishing his business before it became a public limited company. (16 marks)

(6) To what extent did the patent guarantee a profitable future for Ricky? (16 marks)

Total: 80 marks

■ ■ ■

Answer to question 4: candidate A

(1) Limited liability means that the shareholders can only lose the value of their shares. If a business gets into debt its creditors cannot ask shareholders to pay directly. Creditors can force the company to sell its assets, but if this sum is not enough to pay the creditors then they (the creditors) will not receive the full amount owed.

e This is a comprehensive definition of limited liability, showing excellent understanding. Unfortunately, the question asks for its 'significance'. These are touched on in the part about non-payment of creditors, but some explanation of its significance in encouraging shareholders to buy shares is expected. Limited liability reduces risk for shareholders.

(2) The owners of a limited company are the shareholders. In small companies these are often members of the same family or friends.

Limited companies are controlled by the directors. In family firms these will be the owners, and so for most limited companies there is no divorce. However, as companies get bigger it is more likely that ownership is beyond the wealth of a family or group of friends.

e The opening two paragraphs set up the answer nicely. In the second paragraph the candidate starts to explain the divorce.

These shareholders mostly want a financial return — good dividends and increases in share prices — and so they will want directors and managers who are the best. This is not necessarily the people who own most shares.

As companies get larger the divorce increases. With over a million shareholders it is impossible for some companies to be run by their owners. Institutional investors (such as pension funds) buy shares but do not tend to vote at AGMs. They want the best managers to run the firm, but do not get involved otherwise.

e The two final paragraphs would ensure full marks for this answer.

(3) Small businesses cannot afford expensive market research and marketing, especially in the early years. They rely on secondary research through local papers and population statistics. Their marketing is probably word-of-mouth, or a small advert in the local newspaper, on the radio, or an entry in the *Yellow Pages*.

e A good introduction on which to build the evaluation.

For a café this is likely to be enough. It will get its customers from the local area, and it will be very easy to see who and where the competition is. It may even be possible to note the types of firms that are closing down so that you can avoid that type of business. Marketing is much easier too. The target market is in your area and so local adverts can be used. Seeing how other businesses advertise will give the café guidance on how to promote its firm. It might also point up methods that are not used and should be avoided. Niches can be spotted.

e Excellent application to the scenario, with the candidate demonstrating evaluation in the observations on closures and methods to avoid.

Ricky's sticky tape would be much more difficult. It has very limited local appeal and so his marketing would need to be national. It would be hard to persuade large shops like WH Smith to stock his product — besides he would probably not be able to produce enough. His rivals are very large firms, and they will be able to afford much better research and advertising. He was lucky that some local shops agreed to stock it. In fact, all of his sales have come from personal contacts.

e There is evidence of further analysis and evaluation here, with effective use of the information provided combined with the candidate's own thinking.

As a PLC the company will be able to spend money to improve production. Another benefit will be Ricky's chance to market the product nationally.

e The final paragraph adds marginally to the quality of the answer, as the wording does not prevent inclusion of factors relating to the PLC. However, the comment on production is irrelevant.

(4) The first advantage will be the extra money. This will help Ricky to mass-produce or introduce lean production so that he can reduce price.

e This is a good opening, but a major opportunity has been lost through the failure to elaborate on this idea.

As mentioned, extra marketing and research will help him to reach more customers. If the product is as good as it seems, then being a PLC will help the company to make a lot of profit before the patent runs out. He has wasted a lot of time as a sole trader.

e The last line shows good insight but the point made is left in the air somewhat.

A PLC will mean that Ricky can share the workload. Ricky seems to be more of an inventor than a businessman. Specialists can be employed and they will increase productivity. Ricky can specialise in inventing products, or whatever strengths he has. Other employees will bring new ideas into the company too.

e Very good deliberations on the benefits of specialism.

Limited liability is a major advantage. As a sole trader with sales of £0.5m Ricky could end up bankrupt. As a shareholder he can only lose his share value.

e Another critical factor that has been explained briefly, and then placed in context.

question

The major disadvantage is 'independence'. Ricky will now need to think of other people when making decisions. It states that Ricky has 'a fierce desire to be his own boss'. He is still the boss but he might prefer working on his own.

e A well-argued concluding paragraph. Overall, the answer contains a full range of ideas, but more could have been made of them in places.

(5) Typically, start-up problems will fit into four categories: finance, marketing, operational and personnel.

e A useful start, as long as the points are then developed.

(Please see the answer to question 3 for the marketing problems.)

e This is bad practice. Never cross-reference answers — questions 3 and 5 do include some overlap but the contexts are different. Question 3 is a comparison of marketing between two firms. Question 5 concerns problems of start-up for one business. An examiner will not look back two questions to try to find a connection. If you think that an idea is relevant in two questions then you should include it in both, but be careful — this should be a rare occurrence in an examination.

Finance — small firms are short of cash and will find it difficult to survive. It says in the article that Ricky relied on his savings and Gemma's income. This means that he was unprofitable for a long time and would have gone out of business if he had not been able to get money somewhere else.

Operational — it was expensive to produce on a small scale.

Personnel— this was not a problem, as he did not employ anyone.

e The finance section has been covered well, but the other categories have not been explained.

(6) A patent gives its owner a monopoly for about 16 to 20 years. Monopoly means no competition and so this should help Ricky to make a good profit.

e A good opener, but how does monopoly help profit? Sometimes students do not include logic that seems obvious, but an examiner can only award marks for what the candidate includes in the answer.

It is not a guarantee though. In the early years the tape lost money because it was expensive to produce and hard to market. A monopoly can limit competition and this helps a firm to charge a higher price. If the product has no uses, though, it will still not sell. There have been lots of patents that have not made money because they were not commercial (wanted by the public at a good selling price). There may be barriers that stop the inventor from breaking into the market. It would be very difficult to make a brand new car if you had no experience.

e Excellent evaluation of factors that could limit the benefits of patenting.

Another problem with patents is the laws protecting them. Copies are often made and yet the patent does not seem to stop this. In this instance the patent will not guarantee a profit. A slight modification may be enough to get around the patent, even if the basic idea is being copied.

In Ricky's case the chamber of commerce seemed to be important, along with his wife's money. Without their help he would have failed. Luck will always play a part. The PLC should help, but there is no certainty that it will make money.

The patent has only been one factor influencing profit. Mind you, it is better to have one than not.

e A limited ending, but a good observation that does address the question.

e **This is a grade A answer. A few marks would have been lost on question 1, and the answer to question 5 is much weaker than the others because of its limited focus. The other answers are of very high quality and this would be a solid A grade rather than a marginal one.**

■ ■ ■

Answer to question 4: candidate B

(1) Limited liability means that the shareholders can only lose the money that they have put into the business. It applies to private limited companies and public limited companies. As a sole trader Ricky would have had unlimited liability. He could lose his personal possessions.

e An understanding of the term is shown, but as in candidate A's answer its significance is not mentioned. The 8 marks available indicate that more than just a definition is needed.

(2) Shareholders are the owners of a company. They control the company by voting at the AGM. As owners they receive dividends based on the profits. If they think that the company is being run badly they could elect a new board.

e This is a disjointed answer suggesting that the question has not been understood. The candidate has explained a few key words in the sentence in the hope that this is relevant.

(3) Ricky's product would be very difficult to explain. Consumers would not believe that it would work and so they are unlikely to try it. The market research would have the same problems. Customers would say 'yes', it seems like a good idea, but would be reluctant to change brands.

e This is not the approach the examiner would have expected, as the question was intended to compare a local service (with a more easily defined market) to a nationally-sold product that would be harder to market. That said, this approach does show why Ricky's product would be hard to market and so it is relevant.

It might be expensive to buy the special stick. Most people would not imagine that they spend very much on sticky tape and would not want to pay for an unstick

stick, especially if they did not know the company's reputation. It would be useless if the product failed or the company liquidated.

Unfortunately, there is no comparison with the café and so this response does not fully answer the question.

(4) The main advantage would be the additional finance. This would help to produce the tape on a larger scale, and introduce new technology and lean production. They can now compete on equal terms with the large firms. If price is the main factor then this will make their sales increase. If it is not it will still help — they could put up the price, increasing their profit margins. These profits could be ploughed back into the business, making it even larger and more efficient.

Good analysis, with evaluation shown in the comment on whether price is important.

Banks are more likely to lend to limited companies — they can provide more security for loans. Limited liability will help Ricky. He has used up his savings — with unlimited liability he might have lost his house and car, although this could have been prevented if they had been placed in his wife's name. Only those possessions legally owned by Ricky would have been in danger.

The limited liability theme has been handled well, with some sound analysis.

New owners will also help in the running of the firm, and they will bring in new ideas that will improve the firm. The accountant has given Ricky good advice.

A weak conclusion as it stands, lacking supporting evidence.

(5) Cash flow problems are experienced by most new start-ups. Ricky suffered from cash flow problems, despite having lots of savings before he started. When you start you have to spend money on buildings, equipment etc. Suppliers will not give you credit because you have no reputation for paying on time. It is typical also for large firms to delay payment. A good business plan would have encouraged a bank to agree an overdraft, and the main banks have specialists who will advise and help small firms.

A comprehensive opening, weighing up the problems against some factors that would worsen the problem and others that would ease it.

Ricky would need to set up a production plant and so he will need more money than a café, like Alan's. Location is also important. If located at the end of an industrial estate, then it may be difficult to find.

Rather naïve, given the nature of the business. This argument would be applicable to a café though.

If Ricky is the only worker, he will be vulnerable if he is ill. He could not take holidays and his lifestyle could suffer. On the other hand, he does have independence. This is important for him and might override all of the other factors. If

Gemma is in a well-paid job and he has large savings, then he could continue for a long time, but eventually this would be a problem.

e Some excellent evaluation, drawing in issues of lifestyle, his own personal priorities and his family circumstances and their impact on his situation.

If Ricky has employees, is he a good manager? He might find it difficult giving orders or trusting his employees. He did not take any holidays — this might indicate a lack of faith in his staff. If he does not recognise them or give them responsibility, then they will become demotivated. There are not likely to be promotion prospects in a sole trader business.

e A far from elementary deduction that Sherlock Holmes would have been proud to make. This candidate has really got into the business and seems to be answering the questions as if he or she had inside knowledge. This is an impressive skill to demonstrate in an examination.

The finance would be the main difficulty; without it the business would go bankrupt. The other problems would just reduce efficiency.

(6) Patents mean that no one else can make your product. You have a monopoly, meaning no competition. A monopoly can charge whatever price it likes and the customer has to pay.

e This is too narrow. The arguments presented are logical and correct, but stated in too extreme a manner. There is a lack of recognition of a whole host of other possible influences.

Monopoly is the best form of competition for a firm, and with a patent the government will not stop you exploiting the customers as it has given you the monopoly. However, with R&D it may not mean a profit straight away. Once the research has been paid for the business will do very well.

e The final sentence is good. Lack of time may have prevented the student producing a more balanced argument.

e **Overall, this is a grade C set of responses. The answers contain no glaring weaknesses, but the focus of some parts is rather narrow. Question 5 is clearly the best answer, showing the benefit of trying to place oneself in the position of the person or people in the case study. Useful marks are also earned in questions 3 and 4.**

Business objectives

Study the information and answer **all** parts of the question that follows.

Trouble at Typotex

It was just like Animal Farm. The list of corporate objectives had been removed and replaced by a new list. Jo had to agree that the new objectives were expressed clearly and, apart from the fact that nobody else knew that they had changed, they seemed to meet most of the requirements of good objectives.

Typotex PLC had been a considerate employer. The staff facilities were excellent, although the pay was low. Jo had stayed because of the training offered by Typotex — she had developed some important skills in a pleasant working environment.

At times she felt that the workers had it too easy. As a sales person she noticed that the high costs and lack of attention to after-sales service were leading to lower sales. Her feedback was largely ignored — the company was reluctant to introduce more capital-intensive production methods. In part, this was because the new technology required the use of valuable, non-renewable resources from a country that had a poor reputation for human rights.

Jo was less happy with the other reason given — product quality was fine but after-sales problems were caused by incorrect use by customers. Her two main customers had indicated that they were being forced to look elsewhere by their finance departments. 'We no longer have the authority to just choose the best product. Costs and maintenance quality are considered too, and they are your weakness,' confided her contacts.

In fairness, the managing director had immediately agreed to her request for a meeting. He explained the conflict that had occurred at the last AGM. The shareholders had threatened a vote of 'no confidence' in the board if steps were not taken to give their needs greater priority. The shareholders had complained that the company was ignoring their needs in favour of other stakeholder groups. The fall in profit from £100 million to £10 million in 1 year and the directors' forecast of a loss of £20 million for the next year had provoked howls of outrage. Shareholders questioned the wisdom of the company's three stated key corporate objectives which were to:

- produce high-quality products and services
- support, encourage and develop the talents and needs of the company's employees
- maintain the company's reputation as a socially responsible organisation

'What use are these corporate objectives if we cease to exist in the next few years?' queried some shareholders. A compromise had been agreed. In the next 3 years, a series of short-term objectives would be established, with a greater focus on profit and new technology. This new technology would require the use of valuable, non-renewable resources from a country that had a poor reputation for human rights.

(1) Explain the difference between a shareholder and a stakeholder. (8 marks)

(2) Analyse the reasons why a firm such as Typotex would set itself certain objectives. (12 marks)

(3) Evaluate the quality of the original three key corporate objectives of Typotex, in the context of the situation in the text. (15 marks)

(4) To what extent did the actions of the company enable it to meet the key corporate objectives shown in the text? (15 marks)

(5) Evaluate the reasons for a shift from a focus on long-term objectives to short-term objectives, with reference to the situation in the text. (15 marks)

(6) To what extent is it inevitable that the wishes of shareholders will conflict with the aims of the workforce in a company such as Typotex? (15 marks)

Total: 80 marks

Answer to question 5: candidate A

(1) Shareholders buy shares in the firm. If a shareholder has 500 shares in a company with 5,000 shares, then he or she will own 10% of the business and get 10% of the votes. Shares can be ordinary or preference — only ordinary shareholders get votes, with one vote per share. The dividend for ordinary shareholders depends on the profit made.

e This is a comprehensive explanation of shareholders.

Stakeholders have an interest in the firm. It will affect them in some way or other. Examples are trade unions (which will want good working conditions), customers (who want cheap, good quality products) and suppliers (who want prompt payment). Shareholders are also stakeholders.

e A couple of examples would have been enough to guarantee top marks.

It can be seen that different stakeholders have different objectives and this will cause clashes, but most will want a profitable company.

e Full marks would have been earned, but at the expense of some time.

(2) Setting objectives will be useful to Typotex in a number of ways:

- to provide motivation
- to give a sense of direction
- to enable a company to monitor progress
- to assess the success (or failure) of individual staff
- to improve communication

e A good framework for a plan, but there was no need to list all the points before looking at each one individually.

To provide motivation — if staff have a clear target they will work hard to reach that target. This will encourage them to be more efficient and find better ways of doing their job. This can help the firm as it will have an innovative workforce. However, too much innovation may prevent the achievement of a target and so it could be argued that innovation is stifled by objectives — especially if they are very specific and quantitative.

This is an excellent analysis of motivation, with some evaluation of innovation.

To give a sense of direction — individuals and informal leaders may develop in a firm and take decisions that are not in the interests of the company. It is doubtful whether Typotex's objectives were giving clear direction to the workers as they had changed and only Jo knew about it. Good communication is needed to guarantee a clear sense of direction.

The observation about the change of the objectives shows a high standard of evaluation. Full marks have nearly been achieved at this stage of the answer.

To enable a company to monitor progress — objectives must be checked periodically to see if they are being achieved. In this way the managers can learn about their progress. If they are achieving their objectives, then the strategies and tactics being used are obviously successful. If they are failing to meet their objectives, then they can change tactics.

To assess the success of individual staff — if MbO is employed they can see which employees are performing well. These may receive bonuses.

Full marks have been earned by now, and it would be advisable to move on to the next question. Examiners would not expect as many as five different evaluative arguments.

To improve communication — everyone will know what the company wants to do. Constant monitoring of progress will help everyone to understand what the company is aiming to achieve.

Time has been lost — these ideas are not earning any more marks.

(3) The company's three stated key aims were:
- to produce high quality products and services
- to support, encourage and develop the talents and needs of the company's employees
- to maintain the company's reputation as a socially responsible organisation.

The main factors are collated well at the beginning.

Good aims should be SMART — Specific, Measurable, Attainable, Realistic and Timed.

Specific and measurable — the company objectives are much too vague. There is no easy way to judge 'quality' of products and services, and so this first objective is not measurable. Customer satisfaction surveys would help Typotex to assess quality and measure improvements over time.

Very good application of theory to the case, earning evaluation marks.

In the case it states that Typotex's products were good (but expensive). Typotex is poor on after-sales. The company needs to find out what customers see as quality — the company's own view seems to be much too narrow. Then it could set some numerical targets that could be measured.

e **Good judgement is shown here.**

The development of employees seems to be happening ('facilities were excellent') and Jo, at least, was happy — despite the pay. However, there is no way of measuring it.

Maintaining company reputation is another vague target. How can reputation be measured?

Attainable/realistic — all three aims seem to be realistic, but Typotex will need to change its after-sales service if it is to achieve quality. If it loses £20m next year it is doubtful that it could afford to be socially responsible — it has already started to trade with a country with a poor human rights record.

e **More evaluation, based on the link between social responsibilities and profit. Unfortunately, the text has been misread; the firm has not traded with the country with poor human rights, but given the financial crisis at the end of the article the logic can still be applied.**

Timed — none of the objectives is dated. This is useful because it gives a deadline and can help to add realism to the target.

In conclusion, I would say that these are not good objectives. The company itself is being forced to set new objectives, proof that these were unsuitable. They ignore the most important issue in business — profit. With the company about to lose money, it should set a specific profit target, with other objectives based on customers' opinions and so on. The main problems with the original objectives are that they were not measurable or timed and ignored key issues.

e **Conclusions are usually valuable in evaluation questions but on this occasion the earlier answers have made this redundant. In itself, the conclusion is worthy of more credit, but the maximum mark has already been given.**

(4) Any company that changes its objectives without telling the workforce is unlikely to reach its objectives. Communication is vital if a business is to succeed.

The new short-term objectives may, eventually, help them to make more profit, but if there are disagreements it will make it more difficult.

Typotex's treatment of its staff would have helped it to achieve the second objective. The training has persuaded Jo to stay. Herzberg would argue that training will help promotion — a motivator. The pay is not so important as it is a hygiene factor. Workers' jobs were also being protected by the lack of new technology. This was good in the short term but could cost far more jobs if Typotex failed.

e **Good link of theory to the case, allowing analysis and a judgement to be made.**

Customers were unhappy with the company. They judged it on price and after-sales service. Typotex assumed that its product quality (which was good) was the only important factor. In this way it did not meet the customers' needs. However, this

is based on two companies which talked to Jo. This is not a valid sample and it is possible that Typotex was doing the right thing in keeping up quality standards.

e Excellent balanced discussion on whether the quality objective was met, showing a fine sense of recognition of potential uncertainty.

There is evidence to suggest that the company had stopped acting in a socially responsible way. It was using non-renewable resources and investing in an undesirable country. The agreement at the AGM — to focus on profit and new technology — would make it more difficult to look after the needs of the environment and the community, and to protect jobs.

To what extent did the actions of Typotex enable it to meet the three key objectives? I would say that mostly it did not. The products did not suit the customers who wanted cheaper prices and good service, and socially, decisions were not responsible. Only the objective to help workers seemed to be met.

e Again, the length of the answer must be challenged. The answers are excellent but for a candidate displaying this level of understanding there is a dilemma. Can this standard be maintained over all six answers? If it can, then answers that investigate three or four different aspects of a problem in detail are fine. However, in this case it becomes evident that the candidate did not manage time effectively.

(5) In an emergency, desperate measures must be taken. This will help the company to make some money so that it can survive. Without profit it will go out of existence and have no long-term future. Shareholders, worried about their money, will dominate decisions in times of difficulty.

RAN OUT OF TIME!

e The candidate has only managed to write a brief answer. Nevertheless, the marks earned on this question were critical in enabling the candidate to reach a grade B. These few points earned more credit than the final third of the previous answer, because so few marks were still available after the first two-thirds.

e **In effect, this candidate has been marked out of 50 marks (plus a few for question 5). This means that an A grade could not be achieved and yet the first four answers all earned full marks. This student obviously understands business studies but has been reluctant to curtail an answer when there is still more to be said. On occasions this must be done. Plan your time carefully so that you can recognise when to move on to the next question.**

■ ■ ■

Answer to question 5: candidate B

(1) A shareholder owns shares in the business. She would be a part owner.

e The 'explanation' of shareholder is correct, but too brief.

A stakeholder owns lots of shares — more than 50%.

e This is obviously a guess. A reasonable tactic but only if there is enough time. It may have been better to leave space and return to this later (a clue may have emerged in a later question).

(4) The actions that Typotex took did help it to meet the objectives set.

e Omitting questions is a potentially dangerous approach. You could easily forget you'd jumped two questions by the time you completed question 6. Furthermore, there is often a logical structure to the questions, with later questions building on earlier ones. If certain questions prove to be more demanding, it is advisable to modify your time allocation to allow more time for the questions that test your strengths. However, *in a paper where all questions are compulsory it is safer to take them in order.*

It states in the text that Typotex had been a considerate employer and that staff facilities were excellent. The company also offered training. These would have achieved the second objective.

e The approach used for this answer is logical but disjointed. Following the order of the text guarantees relevance, but means leaping from one objective to the other.

It would be better to describe the objective being discussed, rather than referring to its number in the sequence. The examiner may lose the flow of your response if he or she needs to refer constantly to the question paper.

The firm has shown that it cares about its social responsibility because it has refused to trade with a country with poor human rights. This shows that its actions are helping it to achieve its objective, even though it may make it more difficult to make a profit because of the opportunity cost.

e This answer would score well on content, but only the 'social responsibility' element has been analysed.

The product quality was fine and so the first objective is met.

All of these facts prove that the company did meet its objectives.

e Overall, the answer seems to be trying to prove the point and ignores evidence that suggests the opposite — this approach should be avoided for questions which require evaluative responses.

(5) Profits have fallen from £100 million to a forecast loss of £20 million. This has made the shareholders feel worried. They seem to have suddenly discovered that making a profit was not one of the key objectives of the business and so they are making sure that it is given the top priority.

e Excellent evaluation.

While the company was making £100m a year no one would have worried, but if I was a shareholder I would be upset if my shares became worth less because the

business did not want to replace workers with more efficient machines, or buy resources from the wrong country. It would also mean that I did not get my dividend, my share of the profit. My living standard would be affected by this and my savings would be worth less.

In my opinion this is the major reason for the change. Shareholders will be happy to let the business focus on other objectives as they do not always want maximum profits. (They have no way of knowing if it is being achieved, in any case.) As long as a reasonable profit is made they will be happy.

A second idea is then evaluated to a high standard. Words such as 'because' and 'as' are crucial here in continuing the development of the argument. Judgements have been supported by evidence.

Another factor is the need for profit. Without profit firms cannot invest in the techniques that will produce good quality products, or help with socially desirable activities. They must also train their workers. Thus in a crisis, profit becomes the most important target because without it they cannot meet other objectives.

Finally, there is the objective of survival. In a way this is always the most important aim. If survival is threatened, then short-term measures must be introduced. This may mean selling off shops or factories that were helping to achieve objectives in order to get the money to pay debts. Usually this policy would be a disaster, but not if it keeps the business alive, even if it then struggles to make a profit again.

I do not think that the objectives had changed for just the reasons stated. The long-term objectives totally ignored the need to make some money. This seems to be a major omission because all of the other objectives rely on the company being able to afford them. So although the emergency has led to a shift to short-termism, with more emphasis on profit, in the long run they should look clearly at how useful their objectives are.

The candidate shows real insight in the concluding sentences, adding a further view to an already excellent reply.

(6) It is inevitable that shareholders' and workers' needs will conflict. There is a limited pot of money in a firm and both groups will want the lion's share. Workers will demand higher wages and if they see that Typotex is making a lot of profit, they will be in a stronger bargaining position. It depends on whether Typotex could carry on making profit if there was a strike. If Typotex had a lot of stock or new workers could be brought in, then the existing workers would find it more difficult to achieve their aims.

High-quality analysis of the potential conflict.

Workers will also want better working conditions, more training, longer holidays. All of these will cost money and reduce profits.

Shareholders want to make money from the company from higher dividends or share prices. Cutting costs will make more profit and, as wages are a major cost, this will cause conflict because the shareholders will want to cut wages so that more profit is made.

If profit is retained, the share price will go up as the firm is worth more money. A lot of retained profit will go on buying machines — this will cost jobs as workers are replaced. However, it will not always lead to conflict. Those workers who remain may have more enjoyable jobs (machines often do the boring, difficult tasks). The conflict will not be between the workers and the shareholders, but between the ex-workers and the shareholders. All the same, it may leave the current workforce feeling insecure. The loss will add to their insecurity.

e A balance now appears. Earlier fears prove to be unfounded as the potential for agreement between the two stakeholders is explored.

Some people argue that a well-motivated workforce will make a lot of profit for shareholders because workers do their job well. In this case there is no conflict. Shareholders will want the company to spend money on the workers if it means more profit for them. Paying high wages should attract the best workers too.

e The answer could have been applied more fully to Typotex but, given that the term 'stakeholder' was not recognised earlier, this is a good answer.

(3) Typotex's original aims were not very good. As mentioned before, they made no mention of profit and this is why the company is forecast to make a loss.

e The candidate does not seem to have recognised the concept of 'good objectives' from the AS course. However, by reading through the case study carefully he or she has been able to apply logical reasoning to the situation and earned some credit.

Being socially responsible was a big disadvantage. It stopped Typotex from using the new technology that would have helped the firm.

The workers were treated well, but they did not help the customers very much and wanted to avoid responsibility.

I would need more evidence on labour turnover, productivity and absenteeism before making a judgement on how good the objectives were.

e A nice conclusion.

The candidate did not attempt question 2. If the candidate had no understanding whatsoever, then missing it out was a valid approach. However, if the candidate decided to leave it to the end because there was less that he or she could write on the subject, then this was a costly mistake.

e **This is a C-grade script, with excellent answers to questions 5 and 6 being offset against weaknesses in other areas. In places the student applied good sense to areas of uncertainty, but the omission of question 2 and the brevity of question 3 brought down the overall grade.**

Business strategy

Study the information and answer **all** parts of the question that follows.

Lightningtree International

Lightningtree International (LI) was one of Britain's most successful companies. Unusually, in the new millennium it was hard to identify its core business.

John Lightningtree, the founder, had possessed a rare insight into changes in fashion and trends, and always seemed to be one step ahead of rivals in anticipating changes. His daughter, Felicity, had succeeded him as managing director 8 years ago.

Felicity had inherited her father's ability to spot opportunities, but the similarity ended there. John had been a benevolent authoritarian leader. In contrast, Felicity believed in empowering her managers. Under John's leadership each of the 20 separate divisions of the company had needed his approval before making strategic decisions. Felicity was the opposite; she gave full authority to her managers to run their divisions.

There had been some problems. The clothing division was closed down to avoid further losses, and the Licensed Brokerage division caused bad publicity with its overcharging. Felicity judged on results: her managers received high rewards for success; failure led to severe penalties. The success of the remaining 18 divisions was more than adequate compensation.

But things were to change. Felicity's first action as managing director was to place a full-page advertisement in all of the national newspapers announcing a competition for young entrepreneurs. The best ten business proposals and plans would receive full financial backing from LI if the entrepreneurs were prepared to become a part of the company.

That single action transformed LI. Despite the financial strength of the company, the products introduced by her father had not kept pace with the market. Market research conducted on the day that she took control showed that LI products sold mainly to the over 50s. She also experienced problems in encouraging the managers who had served her father to take responsibility for decisions without consulting her first.

The volume, originality and quality of the business proposals that came in response to the advertisement astounded her. Her advisers had warned her that it was too risky to guarantee to support the ten best proposals. In fact, after a painful process of eliminating a number of original ideas, Felicity gave up trying. In the event, an additional 22 divisions (albeit small ones) were added to the company. Overnight, LI was transformed from a company with an ageing management to one with a cohort of young, innovative thinkers.

Felicity had never had a head for figures, but her accountants did. Her claim to be a democratic manager did not apply to new initiatives. Felicity knew that she knew best. Her intuition was inspired and the main role of the accountants was to find ways of raising the finance to support the continual flow of ideas through the company. This tended to be a short-term problem as most of the new divisions were soon profitable.

Felicity had taken over the company just after the last recession. A period of upturn in the business cycle, and her desire to give more freedom to managers, had led to major expansion overseas. 20% of its production and 50% of its sales were now in Europe, and the company was expanding into Japan and the USA. Furthermore, LI employed more new graduates than any other company in Britain.

Some of the divisions that focused on communications were unified to enable LI to offer a full package of hardware, software, communications equipment and systems. This activity contributed 40% of the firm's profits. Such was the success of this area of activity that an investigation was undertaken by the European Union. The result was a hammer blow — LI was deemed to be using its market domination to force customers to pay excessive prices for its equipment. Unless LI could persuade the European Union otherwise, the Commission would take action to split the communications division of Lightningtree into separate companies. Felicity was concerned; they had only adopted these tactics in order to make enough profit to fund the research needed to compete with the American companies which dominated the global market.

Felicity was also worried by the Treasury forecast of a rise in cyclical unemployment and a period of deflation for the next 18 months. What worried her most was the fact that it was not a widespread deflation. All of Britain's main trading partners were expecting a period of inflation.

At a meeting with a government official who explained that the British government was obliged to comply with EU directives, the official assured Felicity that the government would do its best to support LI. She was reassured by his comments about LI's main international rivals: in the USA, the American government was taking no action against US companies' domination of the market. Reflecting back on the conversation, Felicity sat down to consider the case that LI could make in its defence.

(1) Explain *two* factors that would lead to a rise in cyclical unemployment. (8 marks)

(2) (a) What is meant by the term 'deflation'? (4 marks)

(b) Analyse the likely impact of the anticipated period of deflation in the UK on the profitability of LI. (12 marks)

(3) Evaluate the merits of the European Union's proposal to split Lightningtree into separate companies. (16 marks)

(4) Compile a SWOT analysis of LI, and use the SWOT to discuss the future potential of LI to maintain its levels of profit. (20 marks)

(5) On the basis of your SWOT analysis, evaluate the possible strategies that LI could use in order to maintain its record of success. (20 marks)

Total: 80 marks

■ ■ ■

Answer to question 6: candidate A

(1) Cyclical unemployment would be caused by a recession. In a recession there is less output and expenditure, meaning that fewer jobs are needed. All organisations will be affected by cyclical unemployment, but it will be more pronounced in industries that produce luxury products. Consumers will cut back on these first.

A lack of confidence in the future will cause firms to postpone investment plans and run down their stock levels, in case stock cannot be sold. This will then hit

question

firms that make machinery or build factories, leading to unemployment.

A thorough explanation of two factors showing an excellent understanding.

(2) (a) Deflation is when prices fall. Price changes are measured by the RPI. It is quite common for certain prices to fall (e.g. seasonal foods) but, for deflation to occur, most prices would need to follow. It has not happened in Britain for 70 years.

This definition would earn full marks. More importantly, a student who is able to recognise the meaning of terms with such accuracy will be equipped to deal with more detailed questions that rely on good understanding.

(b) If demand falls, firms are forced to cut prices in order to sell products. Thus it would be bad news for LI. Unemployment is caused by deflation. A firm buying raw materials today at £1 will find they are worth 90 pence by the time they are sold. This makes it difficult to make a profit and so firms will cut output, meaning more job losses, lower demand and prices and so on. The multiplier effect will make this problem worse.

Excellent analysis, showing the connection between deflation and profitability.

Deflation will hit luxuries most. The communications division, dealing in luxuries, will lose more profit than the others. Felicity's success has been greatly helped by the growth in the economy. It is therefore probable that it will be badly hit by the recession.

Evaluation, although not directly requested, confirms the quality of the answer. Full marks would have been earned up to this point.

Exports to other countries can be increased in price, as they do not have deflation and with lower costs in the UK these exports will be very competitively priced. If price elasticity of demand is high, this will be very helpful. The opposite will apply if ingredients are imported — they will be more expensive than UK goods.

(3) The European Union's competition policy aims to 'act in the best interests of the consumer'. If LI can offer a package to firms, then it may be cheaper for firms to buy all their items from LI. This could lead to a monopoly if the opposition is forced out of the market. When this happens the producer can charge whatever price it likes, in which case the consumer is not being helped.

Another top class answer. The reasons for the EU concern are explained clearly.

Microsoft has been accused of using its market dominance to make it difficult for people using 'Windows' to access other internet providers. This makes it difficult for other providers to compete, even if their products are better than Microsoft's. This will limit innovation, as Microsoft will not need to improve its product.

An excellent example, further clarifying the candidate's understanding of the topic.

This may be happening with LI, in which case the EU is justified. However, if LI is just being more efficient it would not be in the consumers' interests to break it up.

They could lose economies of scale and synergy, leading to higher prices and poorer service for buyers.

Evaluation is shown here — the candidate states that *if* LI is not acting in the best interest of the consumer, EU intervention would be justified, followed by an alternative scenario in which it would not.

The EU needs to be fair to European producers too. If LI is unable to compete with the USA and Japan, this could mean that these firms take over the European market and exploit the consumers.

Politics and business do not always mix, but the article encourages this line of argument and the answer shows mature judgement.

To protect jobs the EU should not intervene in this case, although I would like further information before deciding. It is making a very high profit — forcing it to cut prices might be a better idea.

The final sentence concludes with a predictable but evaluative conclusion.

(4) SWOT analysis

STRENGTHS	OPPORTUNITIES
• Wide spread of risks • Size and reputation • Democratic leadership — mostly • Risk taking — innovative company • Financial success	• New markets • Upturn in business cycle • Lower prices for exports • Political influence
WEAKNESSES	**THREATS**
• No obvious core business • Some managers afraid to take risks • Risks taken — dangers • Felicity's poor financial management	• European Union investigation • Competition from USA and Japan • Rising unemployment • Deflation

SWOT analysis tends to encourage bullet points. Only content marks (3 marks for this question) can be awarded, as there are no explanations offered. The second part of the answer has not been attempted.

(5) Building on its strengths, the company could continue to spread its risks by diversifying into new activities. Felicity might be able to spot new opportunities, but she needs to be careful. Managers who were very successful during the boom periods may not be so clever as they think. The lack of direct control might mean that it is too late by the time their failure has been noticed. This happened to the two divisions that closed down. If lots of areas were struggling at the same time, they could bring the rest of the firm down.

A solid conclusion. The first argument is presented, analysed and then evaluated.

The policy of democratic leadership will be helpful, as it encourages more ideas — these will create new products and techniques that will help the company to succeed. The high profits being made will be useful in developing new ideas — this will be cheaper than getting a loan.

The company is exporting 50% of its products. The lack of a recession may help here — cheap goods made in the UK can undercut European rivals.

The communications division makes most profit. The most important strategy will be one that keeps this profit. Lawyers who can point out the benefits of a competitive European firm will help it to make profits.

e Subsequent ideas are relevant and indicate the candidate's knowledge and analytical skills, with some judgement shown.

e **This is an A-grade set of answers. Maximum marks would have been earned on the earlier questions, but only a few marks on question 4. The answer to question 5 confirms that the error was one of technique rather than understanding. If time permits it is always worth checking back to see if you have addressed the questions set. You won't be penalised for additional comments that are wrong as errors are ignored, so you've got nothing to lose.**

■ ■ ■

Answer to question 6: candidate B

(1) Unemployment can be caused by a range of factors. New technology has meant people being replaced by machines. Industries like car manufacture have become more capital intensive, causing unemployment. The car industry has also lost jobs because it has been unable to compete.

e This is a general discussion of causes of unemployment. On the principle that irrelevance is not penalised, these points would be ignored.

Jobs are lost because of a lack of spending in the economy. If less money is spent there will be fewer products made and so workers will become redundant and workers will have less money to spend, causing a further cut in demand and even more unemployment. This is known as the multiplier effect.

e This final argument is very relevant and well-argued. Only one relevant content point is made, but the explanation of that point means a high 'application' mark.

(2) (a) Deflation means falling prices.

e Although this is correct, it would not secure full marks — the total mark for the question suggests that some further comment is needed.

(b) Deflation means lower prices. This will attract more customers and so firms will become more profitable. Their expenses will be cheaper because the prices of raw materials, telephones, electricity etc. will also be falling.

e A selective argument, only looking at the favourable aspects of deflation. However, the business logic is good.

This will increase their profit margin and so they will make even more money.

e This earns some credit too, but would have been seen as analytical if the lower selling price had been noted too.

The combination of higher sales and profit margins will mean higher profit.

e This sentence is analytical.

If the pound is falling in value, this will be good because the exchange rate will fall and so exports will become even cheaper, leading to an increase in sales.

e A common error. If prices are lower in Britain, other countries will want to buy more of the currency rather than less, and so the value of sterling increases. A pity because this was a good line of argument to follow.

(3) This would be very unfair. LI has worked hard to get into its position and the EU has no right to interfere. Businesses should be allowed to do what they want. If customers are willing to buy LI's products it should be allowed to sell them. The competition have only themselves to blame. If people see that successful companies are going to be split up, they just won't bother to try to do well.

e The candidate has allowed personal prejudices to dominate this answer, which has led to certain arguments that have not been justified. However, there are quite a few valid suggestions, and even evaluation in the comment on the possible disincentive effect on firms.

It would also be chaotic. This could lead to bankruptcy with thousands of jobs lost, and that would not be in anyone's interests.

e This is too extreme and detracts from a potentially relevant argument.

The American government is doing nothing and the Japanese always stop imports to help their own companies. The EU is victimising Britain again and in the end it will just mean more jobs lost here as the Americans and Japanese take over.

e Despite the prejudice shown, there is enough business studies to earn over half marks, but it is hard to evaluate (show judgement) if your mind is made up beforehand.

(4) LI has a major weakness — it is about to be split up. If this happens it should form a cartel.

Felicity is very good at seeing new market opportunities. This strength should be exploited by carrying out market research to find out what customers want and using this to bring out new products.

LI has a lot of profits and so any new ventures could be funded.

The company might have another competition to find some new ideas. This was very successful 8 years ago. Those ideas may be rather dated and new people may have more understanding of what today's customers like.

The recession is an opportunity too. With lower prices, LI should be able to compete with other countries.

This question has been misinterpreted. Credit can be given for the strengths noted, but most of the remainder is irrelevant. In a search for marks, the opening and closing arguments could earn minor credit.

(5) LI has a major weakness — it is about to be split up. If this happens it should form a cartel.

A brave decision, although it is not advisable to repeat the same answer for two different questions. If the candidate considered that the previous answer was more relevant to question 5, it would have been advisable to change the number from 4 to 5 and slightly amend the answer to address question 5.

Felicity is very good at seeing new market opportunities. This strength should be exploited by carrying out market research to find out what customers want and using this to bring out new products.

LI has a lot of profits and so any new ventures could be funded.

The company might have another competition to find some new ideas. This was very successful 8 years ago. Those ideas may be rather dated and new people may have more understanding of what today's customers like.

The recession is an opportunity too. With lower prices, LI should be able to compete with other countries.

Should the answer to question 4 have been deleted? If there was no time to write another answer to question 4 the answer is 'no'. An answer that has been crossed out will score zero, but if it is not deleted it may pick up some marks. The SWOT part is definitely worth some marks. (In this case the marks earned did help to secure the higher grade.)

Overall, this candidate would have achieved a sound D grade. The approaches were not ideal, but the answers were underpinned by a reasonable understanding of business concepts and an ability to develop a line of argument.